ARE YOU AS CLOSE TO GOD AS YOU ARE TO MY BUMPER?

A COLLECTION OF PERSONAL MEMOIRS ON FAITH

P Edwards

By Patricia Edwards

Copyright © 2013 by Patricia Edwards

All rights reserved. All stories portrayed are based on actual events and people. No part of this book may be reproduced, in whole or in part, in any form or by any means electronic or mechanical, including photocopying, recording, or by any information storage or retrieval system now known or hereafter invented, without written permission by the author, Patricia Edwards.

Scripture quotations are from The New King James Version of the Holy Bible.

Carole Wimmer's poem *When I say I am a Christian* on page 100 is reprinted with permission by Carole Wimmer.

Manufactured in the United States of America
ISBN: 978-1-4675-6521-9

To purchase this material and others, please visit:

www.patriciaedwardsbooks.com

Are You As Close To God As You Are To My Bumper?
Edited by Randy Peyser – CEO of Author-One-Stop;
Joanne Shwed, CEO of Backspace Ink;
Crystal Trigg, Susan Scott Meredith, and
Dianne Kidwell
Cover design and typesetting by Susan Scott Meredith
Printed and bound by Strategic Print Solutions, Haymarket, VA

To my children

Dave, Dan, and Laura

It wasn't until God graced me with motherhood that I truly understood the real meaning, depth, and substance of love.

Thank you for being my children and my inspiration to reach for the stars and live out my dreams as much as I encourage you to reach for and live out yours.

I love you all always!

Mom

IN LOVING MEMORY OF

Todd Crawford

Jayne Rager-Valseca

Barbara Beck

and

Joanne Rozyczko

ACKNOWLEDGMENTS

First and foremost, I thank our Lord, Jesus Christ, for bequeathing me the task of this book. The journey in its evolution has enriched my soul and deepened my faith, respect, and love for God, life, and people beyond measure.

To the men and women whose lives are unveiled within this context, I am forever in debt to your generosity in making this book come to fruition. I can only imagine how pleased God is with your willingness to boldly speak and share with the world the various ways a relationship with Him can come about and what it consists of. With God, there is a difference in life and it is a wonderful one.

To my parents, thank you for your unwavering support. Both of you have always been here for me no matter the path I have walked. I love you very much.

To my family and friends, thank you for the gifts of encouragement and inspiration.

CONTENTS

Chapter 1	Even though I walk through the valley of the shadow of death, I will fear no evil for You are with me	1
Chapter 2	It is what it is	15
Chapter 3	I revealed Myself to those who did not ask for Me, I was found by those who did not seek Me	26
Chapter 4	Thou wilt keep him in perfect peace, whose mind is stayed on Thee, because he trusteth in Thee	36
Chapter 5	As in mind, so in manifestation	50
Chapter 6	God is within	59
Chapter 7	Each one should use whatever gift he has received to serve others, faithfully administer God's grace in its various forms	66
Chapter 8	If you ask it in My name, I shall do it	72
Chapter 9	For He made Him who knew no sin to be sin for us, that we might become the righteousness of God in Him	80

Chapter 10	And we know that in all things, God works for the good of those who love Him, who have been called according to His purpose	86
Chapter 11	For we are God's handiwork, created in Christ Jesus to do good works which God prepared in advance for us to do	99
Chapter 12	Whoever lives in love lives in God and God in them	108
Chapter 13	Those who wait on the Lord shall renew their strength. They shall mount up with wings like eagles. They shall run and not be weary. They shall walk and not faint	118
Chapter 14	Trust in the Lord with all your heart and lean not on your own understanding; in all your ways acknowledge Him and He shall direct your paths	125
Chapter 15	It is more blessed to give than to receive	131
Chapter 16	Everything comes by faith	142
Chapter 17	God is good in both His love and His justice	158
Chapter 18	There is a time for everything, and a time for every purpose under the heavens	166
Chapter 19	A man of disbelief is at the mercy of a man with a Testimony – **About the author**	173

*Jesus was not sent to normalize sin,
He was sent to eradicate it!*

1

> Even though I walk through the valley
> of the shadow of death,
> I will fear no evil for
> You are with me
> (Psalm 23:4)

The man you are about to meet, Dave Gambale, was one of the most stubborn, smug, and arrogant men on this planet with an ego to match. Through the Holy Spirit's prompting in the course of his rigid and unyielding thinking, Dave received unwavering proof that God's Will is bigger than his own and He turned Dave's life around for him.

The middle child of three, Dave grew up in a rather lax home with easygoing parents. Strict in comparison were his grandparents and he credits their Italian heritage and strong Roman Catholic beliefs for their narrow viewpoints, attitudes, and values.

Regardless of his parent's religious encouragement, it was his grandpa's actions that spoke volumes to him on religion, faith, obedience, exemplification and structure. Inside his grandparent's home was an altar at which his grandpa would kneel and pray every day, especially before bedtime.

In spite of the religious applications of attendance, worship, confession, prayer, schooling, and encouragement during his adolescence, a personal relationship between God and Dave had not formed. In fact, these heart-filled and soul-filled applications of Godliness were equal in significance to getting dressed in the morning or brushing his teeth. Dave went through the motions, no more and no less. Then, a personal incident between his father and their church broadened, mitigated, and lessened any chance of God bridging the gap between Him and Dave's heart for many years.

During the birth of Dave's younger sister, his mother almost died due to hemorrhaging. The doctors advised his parents to refrain from having any future children so, the next time they were intimate, his father cautioned himself. In doing so, this act of 'protection' not only safeguarded her life and guaranteed no more children would be added to his offspring of three, but it also broke the Catholic Church's law on birth control.

(The Catholic Church views contraceptives as wrong because it was a deliberate violation of the design God built into the human race, often referred to as "natural law." The natural law's purpose of sex is procreation. The pleasure that sexual intercourse provides is an additional blessing from God, intended to offer the possibility of new life while strengthening the bond of intimacy, respect, and love between husband and wife. The loving environment this bond creates is the perfect setting for nurturing children.)

As an act of accountability, Dave's father humbly attended "The Sacrament of Penance and Reconciliation," commonly called "Confession" - the method by which an individual may be absolved from sins committed after receiving the sacrament of Baptism. According to Catholic teachings, the person seeking forgiveness must tell his or her sins directly to an ordained Catholic priest or bishop and then the priest or bishop recites prayers of absolution to forgive their sins.

Appallingly, what Dave's father received in return for his confession was far from prayers of absolution. The priest who took his confession proclaimed eternal punishment on his life. Shocked, devastated, and emotionally crushed at the priest's decree, outrage consumed his soul and in return, he cursed the priest who cursed him.

From that day on, church was never approached with the love, joy, and pride that the family once had for it. The only time they stepped into the church was for Easter, Christmas, or Dave's altar boy responsibilities; but even then, they departed immediately after communion. Dave stated, "Home was home, but it didn't feel much like a home because my dad was never around much after that. He was there," Dave pointed to his heart, "but, he really wasn't." Sadly, his parents later divorced.

Irrespective of how much he revered his grandparents, this incident along with a few others made Dave regard people of faith as weak minded individuals. With arrogance, he would mock under his breath and taunt, "Need God? I don't need anyone!"

Dave developed serious aggression issues. He disrespected everyone outside of his family and successfully played the role of "bully". He picked fights all the time even over the simple glance of a "wrong look" that came his way. Needless to say, he spent most of his time alone.

Shortly after high school, he joined the Marine Corps; a fierce and effective military force programmed in their chain of command. Marines take pride in God, the Corps, their country, their enthusiasm, their gung-ho attitudes, and themselves. Dave successfully flourished in this structure to the rank of Sergeant. Regardless of his responsibilities and command, one quality remained missing in Dave's composition as a Marine: God.

During his 20-year tenure as a Sergeant and Drill Instructor, Dave and a few other commanding officers took a platoon of new recruits out into the field for a one-week training expedition. They joined several other platoons in training as well. Included with the staples of tents, cots, food, and water were boxes of "Field Bibles" and Dave's platoon was in charge of them.

Never having participated in Marine worship ceremonies or respect for those who did, Dave often jeered at the boys who attended such services by referring to them as punks and other degrading names. Despite his knowledge that such behaviors as a Marine, leader, brother, and teammate were wrong, he never cared.

When Saturday approached, Dave had the single-handed command of the platoon. With superiority, he informed his recruits that he would answer whatever questions they had about the Corps after they trained well, set up camp, and if he was in a good mood. By dusk, the platoon performed every duty Dave commanded. He was more than pleased and in high spirits.

To keep his recruits busy, he further instructed them to build a bonfire and a seat for him, much like a throne for a king. In no time, both tasks were completed; yet, the element of 'fire' was missing due to a lack of kindling. As Dave sat upon his throne and contemplated ways to start the fire, he looked down, noticed the box of Field Bibles and ordered the Bibles to be burned. Immediately, one recruit, stood up and requested permission to speak. With permission granted, the recruit respectfully informed Dave that he was a born again Christian and he would not witness nor participate in a Bible burning.

This was the first time that Dave had ever heard the words "born again" or "Christian" describing a follower of Jesus. Within seconds, an overabundance of disdain filled his heart. Dave thought to himself, "No one, not some punk kid, is going to tell me what he's not going to do!" In turn, Dave ensured the Bible burning only not as originally planned with the entire platoon; instead, he ordered this boy, this born-again Christian, to burn every single Bible by himself.

Back at the base and days later, Dave's commanding officer arrived at his room and relieved him of his duties because he was under investigation for the for the burning. Dave learned that the recruit whom he had forced to burn the Bibles wrote a letter home about the event. The boy's father then contacted his local Congressman who subsequently contacted the Marine Corps. Dave claimed that he never meant the burning as a sacrilegious gesture. To him, the Bibles were just paper. All of the other recruits who had witnessed the event testified that Dave never said anything good or bad about God or Satan and that they believed his decision to burn the Bibles was not a personal one.

The military investigation concluded that the charges made against him were inconclusive and unfounded. Therefore, Dave was permitted to return to his base, his rank, and his platoon just in time for their graduation.

On graduation day, when valediction was over, the "born again" recruit and his father both walked up to Dave to greet him. Dave shook their hands and immediately apologized for offending them. The boy's father replied, "It's okay, I'm the pastor of a 3,000 member church and we have been praying for you every week."

There is no doubt in Dave's mind today that those prayers combined with the conviction he was under were the true beginnings of change in his life.

God blessed Dave with Chasey, his wife. He stated that he wanted to marry her the moment he saw her. Into their union, they each brought a child from a previous relationship and together, they produced two more children. While marriage softened Dave, he was still far from God and his temper was still out of control. With shame, Dave shared another soul-shaping memory that came the hard way.

Dave coached their son's youth baseball team. Interaction with these kids meant interaction with their parents, a mix of local adults that included Dave's fellow Marine brother, Doyle. Not knowing any other method, Dave coached these kids much the same way he coached his Marine recruits. He yelled, screamed, and cursed at them. In fact, at one game, Dave yelled to Doyle's son, "Hey Dustin! Come here you little ...!" Disgusted and fed up with his verbal explosions, Doyle's wife got up from her seat and left the field. This incident was just one of his many aggressive outbursts.

In the course of their marriage, Chasey rededicated her life to Jesus. She attended church regularly, joined the choir, participated in study groups, and steadily led their children to the mercy, salvation, and redemption of Jesus Christ. As faith grew in Chasey's life, discomfort grew in Dave's.

Determined to resist and live life the way he always had, Dave spent less time with his family and more time with his friends, the *good old boys*.

To find solace in this time of transition, God graced Chasey with 'His' patience. At one point, she and the kids invited Dave to their church block party where worship services were held in a relaxed and fun manner outside. Out of appeasement, Dave agreed to attend.

He roared in on his motorcycle, found his family, walked the grounds, and met a lot of people. Through the crowd, one man in particular stood out from the rest. His name was Denny, and he oddly resembled Dave in appearance. Like Dave, he was stocky, tattooed, and rode a motorcycle.

Now, one would have thought that the introduction between the two men would have been readily received, but instead it was graceless, ill-mannered, and rude - by Dave that is.

With joy and sincerity, Denny politely extended his friendship to Dave and even mentioned that they should ride together sometime. Taken aback at the suggestion, Dave sarcastically replied, "I don't ride with holy rollers."

Buoyant, Denny smiled, handed Dave his business card and encouraged him to call if he ever changed his mind or just wanted to talk. Dave took Denny's card, shoved it inside his wallet, and left the church grounds.

Dave and Chasey's marriage eventually reached a breaking point.

One evening, on his way home, Dave received a call from his wife. She told him that she wanted a separation because they were not equally yoked and she was tired of emotionally living alone. Like his father, Dave was there but really wasn't. Dave referred to that day as the 'darkest day in his life'. All he thought about was how he had failed at a relationship again.

While he drove, his mind raced with ideas as to what he could do and to whom he could call for help. He knew that he and his wife were not equally yoked, but he did not want to lose her. He dug into his back pocket, pulled his wallet out, and found Denny's card.

He called, "Denny, this is Dave Gambale. I don't know if you remember me, but I need to talk to you..." Although their conversation was brief, Denny felt prompted to see Dave immediately, and when Dave pulled into his driveway at home, Denny was there waiting. The two men greeted each other and walked inside.

Quite surprised to see Denny, yet quick to piece the scenario together, Chasey locked her eyes in on Dave and firmly stated, "It won't help."

Denny placed his hand on Dave's shoulder and nudged him to lead them into another room where they could talk privately. For four hours, these two men discussed what a relationship with Jesus Christ looked like and how it worked. Dave learned that it was not exactly as he had imagined and refrained from. When the conversation was over, Dave willingly surrendered his life to Christ.

The following Sunday, Dave attended church with his wife and children, and when the altar call was announced, he stepped forward in front of the entire congregation and he confessed his sins and professed his faith.

One of the many people to witness his conversion was Doyle, his fellow Marine and baseball parent. At the end of the service, Doyle walked up to Dave, congratulated him, and said, "When the service was over, I phoned my wife and told her that she was not going to believe who came up for the altar call today. After I told her that it was you, she asked me if the walls were still standing."

Dave's newfound relationship with Christ taught him to humble himself in his marriage as the leader and to walk alongside his wife while always recognizing both their individuality and union. Knowing what he knows now, Dave credits God for the good fortune of his wife and kids. His marriage is now anchored, centered, and dependent upon God's desires, wants, and expectations of their covenant. Have there been trials since? Yes, but they are not as intense as they once were. Now God is their arbitrator.

Dave views Chasey as his better half, the half that softens his rough edges and compliments his imperfections. He respects her, loves her, and will do anything for her and the kids even if it costs him his life. In fact, whenever he hears these song lyrics, "Those whom you embrace feel the Kingdom and those who are around you are blessed," Dave thinks of her.

Until his conversion, Dave never saw Chasey in this light due to his own distorted ways of thinking and taking her for granted. Now that he has God, he acknowledges that she is a monumental blessing in his life and when he looks at her, he stands back in complete awe that she is even with him and has put up with his shortcomings for so long.

Through Christ, Dave has also discovered someone who truly understood the pains, problems, and temptations that he has battled. He discovered the constant availability of a father who has never abandoned him; he discovered the ointment that filled every vacant space within his and soothed his soul and; he discovered God's grace, undeserved care, and unearned favor that not only saved him from sin, but a defeated life.

As a Marine, Dave knows the meaning of teamwork.

A team consists of several people aligned with one purpose all of whom sacrifice their individual gain for their team's greater good. In doing this, they possess the power to formulate a force that makes the impossible, possible and isn't it the impossible we often want to accomplish in God? Fellowship involves teamwork.

As Christians, we are to go beyond the simplicities of showing up for service or Bible study. We are to hold each other accountable with encouragement, support, love, celebration, and liability regardless of how uncomfortable it may be at times. We must do what we can for the betterment of God, each other, and everyone in which we come into contact. This is how we grow in faith and correct our walk whenever we stumble. If anyone of us falls short or struggles with a stronghold, which most of us do, we are all obligated through Christ to help one another rehabilitate rather than point, judge, argue, or turn our backs.

As Christians, not only are we to focus on our relationship with Jesus, but also on our relationship with others. Only through like minds, paralleled hearts, and shared morals can our ability to walk the talk and lead by example be accomplished.

Dave seeks, calls, and aches for a ministry of true Christian fellowship where we encourage, sharpen, and love one another no matter what. He said, "It would do a world of good for believers to connect whether or not a person has tattoos, chews, smokes, and drinks; who is homeless, is a millionaire, rides a motorcycle, or drives a BMW."

Now, Dave is into the whole "God thing" because it works!

The most indispensable element connecting you to God is prayer. Dave begins his mornings and ends his evenings with prayer ensuring dependency upon Him, not himself. His prayers consist of thankfulness, praise, and petition for others in need.

Dave makes no jokes about it; faith is hard! Especially in today's society where so many others don't understand it. He knows what others are thinking because he used to think like them. To corroborate this claim, he shared other events in the early stages of his faith.

In 2009, Dave struggled with some extraordinarily powerful strongholds in his life. As judgments and rejections flooded in from all directions, including a few fellow believers, he literally closed himself inside his bedroom closet. On his hands and knees, he fought his relationship with God. He testified that as he wrestled the emotional pain that consumed his mind, he felt God wrap His arms around him, hold him, and repeatedly tell him, "I love you, I love you, I love you."

This penetrating message of love made the giving up and handing over of his personal dilemmas to God serene and complete which further validated that all strength and power only comes from the Holy Spirit, not by our own personal efforts no matter how honorable.

God has blessed Dave and his family beyond measure, expectation, or imagination. The Holy Spirit pours immense peace, joy and love into all their lives.

He remarked, "Go to God with your pains, frailties, weaknesses, and strengths. Be honest and be real because when you take the time to open yourself, speak, and lay all your cards out on His table, you walk away with a sense of freedom. Learn to trust Him, and do not feel scared or intimidated about what to say. God already knows your heart, needs, and secrets.

The Lord blesses everything Dave sets his hands to do when his focus is on pleasing Him. Of these blessings, the greatest is love.

Dave is able to feel his children's love for Christ and to be around them is beautiful. The love of God is sensed.

Through the efforts of both Dave and Chasey exemplifying Christ in and around their lives and children, Dave shared some fond memories with their son, Boston. They involve prayer, salvation, and a spiritual growth spurt that stretched his mind, heart, and soul.

Whenever Dave would pray with Boston, Boston held onto his daddy's thumbs while Dave's hands were poised in prayer position. Not only was this cute, it was bonding for both of them.

One afternoon when Boston arrived home from school, he asked his mother if all good people go to Heaven. Chasey told her son that the only way for a person to get into Heaven was through the offering and receiving of salvation. Upon hearing this, Boston informed his mother that he wanted salvation.

That evening, as Dave tucked Boston into bed, they got ready to pray. Boston reiterated to his father that he wanted to pray for salvation. Dave called Chasey into the room and together, they witnessed their son accept Jesus Christ into his life.

Then, when Boston became a member of 'The Royal Rangers', one of America's largest Christian boy's mentoring programs at their church, Dave's own faith increased. To earn a badge within this group, Boston had to memorize a Psalm. He chose Psalm 23. Dave helped him every day, and by the third night, Boston had it down verbatim.

Later that night, Dave returned to his own bed and was half asleep when he heard God say, "That was real good Dad. Your son memorized it; you even taught him to memorize it, but you don't know it. Humble yourself, go back to your son, and ask him to help you." The next night, Boston helped Dave memorize it.

Just as each psalm is as individual as the author themselves, they are all universal. Meaning, they speak and echo the same familiar circumstances, attitudes, views, and spiritual dispositions that many of us face today. And, when it comes to Psalm 23, religious scholar, Bernard Anderson, best described its command when he wrote, "No single psalm has expressed more powerfully man's prayer of confidence "out of the depths" to the God whose purpose alone gives meaning to the span of life, from womb to tomb."

We know that we are never complete without God and that God provides for us, covers us, helps us, and takes care of us. When we stumble, God takes the hit for we are His people. In the end, we learn to work with God, to be good and to expect more of ourselves than others.

So, if you stumble or experience doubt, do not give in or give up. Instead, pray and read psalms. They are one of the most treasured pieces of Scripture in the world where we find humanity at the footstool of holiness.

Dave's life has drastically changed for the better. Now, whenever he sees a cross or a flag, he remembers how he feels about his nation, his fellow Marines, his family, and the God he had once ignored.

Words of Encouragement

"You will never feel the complete sense of love and peace that you internally crave until you reach out and have a relationship with Jesus. Until you open yourself up and get to know God, you truly have no idea what kind of gift He gives you. So, stop being so stubborn! You have nothing to lose, but everything to gain."

- **Dave Gambale**

2

It is what it is

~~~~~

While the old cliché, "It is what it is", can sound a bit callous to some folks, it resonates the strength of one word to Charles' heart and mind. The word is, "Acceptance" - the willingness to tolerate a situation, without complaint, no matter how difficult or unpleasant knowing that we are truly never in control of circumstances and people around us.

Charles Moorer was born the third eldest child of nine in Orangeburg, South Carolina. The family later moved to Bronx, New York where he and his siblings were raised.

A family of this size made the periodic sibling rivalries along with each of their personal wants and needs sometimes difficult. Through their ups and downs, one sure thing stood firm, his mother. Her love and guidance always steered her children to a state of gratitude and appreciation for what they had along with their individual gifts and abilities. This realization minimized their troubles whenever they had them.

Between the ages of seven and 15, Charles intermittently attended services between a Baptist Church where he lived and a Catholic Church where his cousins lived. The ambience and practice between the two denominations were vastly different.

The Catholic Church was dimly lit, the windows were stained, mass was conducted in Latin, and the act of confession frightened him the most. All in all, an unfortunate barrier between the Word and Charles' heart was generated.

The Baptist Church was just the opposite. Bright and luminous with clear sided windows, services were spoken in English which created a profound attachment between the Word and Charles' heart.

As one might imagine, Charles' beliefs were divided between the two practices of faith, but as he matured, his beliefs became a synthesis of the two. No matter where he attended a church service, Charles enjoyed and digested the Word of God. In fact, he and some of his friends founded a church choir called, "The Young Samaritans." Aside from singing in church, they sang on their street corners and they strived to live righteously by visiting the sick and helping the elderly with laundry or grocery shopping.

Charles stated that someone once told him that the two greatest things a person can have in life are faith and belief in God.

Initially, these two qualities were slow for Charles to obtain because he questioned everything much like he does today. He stated, "When you can find an answer to something, anything, you have a clear and a firm understanding that solidifies your position and what you feel. There's no doubt whatsoever. When it comes to God, a person should seek Him in order to find Him."

To better understand this claim, Charles illustrated two variances about the earth and its inhabitants. He said, "The Bible informs us about creation in Genesis 1:14, 'And God said, "Let there be light ..."'" Scientists inform us about the Big Bang Theory, an explosion that resulted in the creation of the cosmos and such. I suggest that we have both: God created the Big Bang."

Charles affirmed that while science can explain some things, it cannot explain everything. He referred to the unexplainable things as "the God factors." "As we grow older, we learn that certain axioms are true – not because we repeated them so often, but because they are consistent." He clarified, "I have developed consistency regarding my belief. Over the years, I have heard some flowery rhetoric and effusive language regarding faith, but nothing is more powerful than the simple words, 'I believe.' I have learned that it is not the extent to which one believes. Either someone believes or they don't. The superlatives more and less do not apply to belief for there is no tool by which one can judge how much another believes."

Considered the guidebook to life, the Bible shepherded Charles on how to live life and treat others substantiating that life is a gift from God and we are not to abuse it or each other. Although a good majority of us today know the correct things to do to maintain respect, love, and kindness in our lives and relationships, quite often we allow another person's experiences, peer pressures, and sometimes politics to get in the way of our character.

God equipped Charles with a core set of principles that not only taught him to recognize the frailties and commonalities we all have with one another, but they have had a positive effect on his role as a husband, father, brother, and friend. He explained, "We do not exist in vacuums or silos. We are connected to those whom we like and dislike; and, we don't form all relationships on our own. Occasionally, people and events are presented in our lives as a test. These tests are catalysts that lead us to places we might not otherwise go, such as an emotion, an opinion, a choice, a reaction, or a physical location."

Charles shared two awful, yet prevailing events in his life where testing and God were at the forefront, although neither one was perceived until much later.

A high school dropout by choice, not failure or indolence, Charles joined the U.S. Army in July 1964. Although the Vietnam War was raging at the time, the veracity of becoming a soldier never entered his mind until he signed the dotted line. With laughter, Charles stated that his mother always had a lot to say whenever she witnessed one of her children on the brink of ruining their lives. And, in this case, she said a lot to him.

Charles stated that when he joined the army, he emotionally escaped the shame of being a high school dropout. While there, he attained his General Educational Development certification.

He survived the Vietnam War, and in June 1967, he received an honorable discharge. Without a plan for his future, Charles floundered and fell into the wrong crowd during the midst of a drug epidemic in New York City. Succumbed to drugs himself, he reeked of foulness.

He always wanted to do the right thing, but he grabbed at the potential to make money – huge money – even when it meant illegal money. He had no one to guide him and the phrase, "misery loves company" seated itself very near to his heart. His first arrest began in June 1968, and others followed until 1972.

Charles compared his life to the 14th-century epic poem, *Inferno* by Dante Alighieri, as he spiraled down to a hell of his own creation. He lived in a world where everything seemed solvable with narcotics because they blinded him to his transgressions and the damage he caused to himself and to those around him – especially his family.

Caught up in the madness of lies, drugs, pleasures, and self-centeredness, Charles didn't care or worry about anything. Constant inebriation numbed him. However, because his drug-induced insanity was a choice and not a biological disorder, it meant that his life could be interrupted and possibly, changed. His incarceration in 1972 was that interruption.

As he served his time, Charles kept himself out of trouble. One evening, he looked out of his cell window and saw a mother deer with her doe grazing under a tree on a hilltop. The image framed its way through his window much like a tranquil painting and it stirred his soul to the truth: Unlike people, animals do not lie and they live with whatever God gives them. This epitome made Charles think, "I'm certainly not an animal, but I definitely haven't been living with what God gave me: the *choice* to be good and to do right."

In that moment, confinement felt more like a house conversion. He remembered that God is found in all things, even in hopeless circumstances. Later that night, while he waited to be counted by the guard, Charles perceived a calming effect, much like a balm, come over him. The moment was so powerful that it soothed and released his desire for drugs. He said, "For the first time in years, my mind was free. I was able to examine my life clearly and analytically."

The saying, 'God will never give you more than you can handle,' is true. Charles served his remaining sentence without incident. He attended church, sought forgiveness, and became moral.

In January 1973, he was released. Back in society, Charles focused on being the productive man he knew God made him to be.

The other "God factor" occurred on August 3, 1979 when death - the great intruder - cast Charles, his mother, and their entire family into a select community that they were not prepared for: a community of loss, sorrow, and void. Charles' younger brother, Eric, was murdered at the age of 15.

What unnerved Charles the most was how the news of Eric's death was delivered to him. His mother's young neighbor, Charlene, phoned him at his Brooklyn home and frantically announced, "Your brother Eric is dead, and your mother is with him!" Then, she hung up.

Charles knew that her intention was to do the right thing, but the manner in which she delivered the message emotionally destroyed him. Shocked and confused, a mad rush of emotions ran through his mind landing him in the pit of intense rage. His next thought was for revenge. Someone had killed his brother, and he was going to kill them.

Prepared to spend the rest of his life in jail, Charles grabbed his .357 Magnum handgun, loaded it, and headed to the subway on a mission to find his brother's killer. The normal hour-long ride on the subway from his Brooklyn home to the Bronx seemed almost instantaneous. Charles hardly remembered the ride itself, but he remembered that everywhere he stepped, people moved and gave him a wide berth. He stated that his facial expression and demeanor must have shouted, "Get out of my way!"

In the Bronx, he took a cab to his mother's home and met up with sweet Charlene. She informed him that his mother was in the Sheffield Houses with Eric. Charles walked there in a daze, almost outside of his own existence as if someone else had control of him.

Once in the apartment, all he saw were police officers swarming around with cameras, note pads, and crime tape. Off in the distance, he heard his mother's sobs. He made his way to her.

As he approached, he absorbed the visualization of his brother's lifeless body lying on the bed where he took his last breath. Eric's eyes were partially closed, and an expression of agony had etched itself onto his mouth. With no pretense in hiding his anger and a loaded .357, Charles just stood frozen.

A moment later, he walked over and stood next to his grieving mother. Then, from out of nowhere, the mission for retribution unexpectedly and suddenly ceased. A higher calling of selflessness entered both his mind and his heart as the divine qualities of composure, calm, retreat, and acceptance came over him. Charles became the pillar of support and strength that his mother needed more than ever.

A moment later, the police captain walked up, placed his hand on Charles' shoulder and said, "Take your mother home. We'll handle this."

The loss of his brother was the greatest moment of grief for both him and his mother. There were no words to express her pain then or now.

Charles professed, "No parent should outlive their child. When a child is tragically lost, the natural order of the universe is out of balance. Back then, I felt that God was testing me, my mother, and our family. With what, I'm not sure. I'm sure if you spoke with each and every one of my family members, they would give a different answer to that question. One thing for sure was this: our grief was proportioned to our loss – no more and no less. We survived the pain knowing that God doesn't give a person more than they can handle, and if it could have been another way, it would have been.

Charles stated, "Though I acknowledge Eric's death as a time of immense suffering and struggle, I also acknowledge it as a time of blessing. Not only did my family and I remember that God is in control of events at every stage, but we became more appreciative of each other and of life in general. So, we cried and we laughed at the times we all had with him and we each missed him in our own way."

Charles' personal trials and tribulations have firmly brought him to the conclusion that no one lives life in a smooth or straight line from Point A to Point B only to finish with the result of success and recognition of God. Instead, all of humanity experiences moments of psychological and spiritual highs and lows, twists and turns, transitions and timeouts all while continuously moving forward, much the way a leaf blows in the wind, metaphorically speaking. He concluded, "While the result to each and every predicament can sometimes be gentle, abrupt, comfortable, or uncomfortable, it will only be revealed on God's term and timing. The question is, "Will we recognize Him when it happens?"

On this topic, existentialists may want to assert that a person could not have escaped their fate or that they were doomed to wind up where they did because they are free individuals responsible for their own actions. Charles begs to differ. "God knows what He has planned for us and there is no way of escaping His will regardless of the erratic choices and experiences we encounter." He willingly accepts this fact with no regrets because without God and the benchmark of consequences in his life from his past, he would not be who he is today.

Charles went on to reveal two theoretical reasons why trust and belief in God can be a challenge or impediment for some people. He explained, "Western religions have a streak of rationalism to them because many things can be explained by science. Unfortunately, this marginalizes God. Then, we have one of the biggest hindrances to man: our superficiality - another crutch for our insecurity. Rather than saying to the world, 'Hi, I'm John and leaving it at that, we go on and on about how much money we make, what we're buying, what we've bought, what we drive, or how big a house we have.

Tooting our own horn is actually a symbolic gesture of an 'act' in order to have an identity which is equivalent to a small child hiding in a closet crying. The behavior is not pure. It's an act of pronounced materialism, and there's nothing good or godly about it."

The toughest lesson with the greatest reward has been to not judge others. Whenever Charles hears someone critique, condemn, or judge another person undeservingly, he politely yet firmly places the faultfinder into their victim's shoes by asking them what they would do if they were in the same situation or that person themselves.

As for vengeance, it truly belongs to the Lord and no one else. God gives and God takes. God allows us the freedom to choose to live rightful or wrongful lives. Quite often, the wrong decisions are examples to others of how not to live.

For humanity as a whole, Charles' philosophy is quite simple: "If you can't help, then do no harm." This is not an impossible task. Give what you can, and remember that quality is the key, not quantity."

In man's earliest history, cooperation was critical to survival. Nowadays, our lives are much easier through the invention of technology and the harnessing of our brain power. We are no longer as closely bound to our neighbors as we used to be and that disconnectedness has led to human tragedy on a scale unimaginable.

Unfortunately, too many of us today are what Charles referred to as "Crisis Christians." That is, we love to treat and look out for those who are less fortunate when there's a crisis instead of exemplifying this quality in our character every minute of every day with everybody, crisis or not.

God calls us to live and behave as if every man, woman, and child are our brother and sister deserving of unconditional love and affection. Not just when they are in crisis, but every day! And these days, many men and women forget that they are equal upon entering into a relationship. They give up equality by choice, not by custom. Could this be why there is so much self-centeredness in relationships and the world? Perhaps, but only through a true abiding relationship with Christ do the blessings of honesty, trust, loyalty, and commitment get poured into our other relationships, especially with a spouse.

Charles acknowledged that regardless of all his efforts at being a good person and a good Christian, he will never become pure, holy, or holier than God because he has done much to taint his soul. He is however, liberated, renewed, and saved from his transgressions because he has held himself accountable, sought forgiveness, and asked for redemption – all possible only through Christ.

He wakes up every day happy with what he has done the day before. The most he may have done to ever possibly fall short was forget to compliment his wife, praise her cooking, rub the dog, and maybe he may have drank too much wine.

All of us who strive to be obedient will, in fact, fall short from time to time. It's normal and it's expected because we are human. So, don't beat yourself up when you stumble. Just learn and improve because it's all part of the growing process of faith.

God gives 'life' so we will find meaning, value, and purpose. God allots 'time' so we will get to know Him, modify who we are, and change the world around us. God allows 'pain' so that we will know love and good choices; and, God gave His son, 'Jesus', to save us from ourselves.

Words of Encouragement

"Do you believe in God? If not, do! This is not a polite request. It's a demand. You can't go through this life not believing. Disbelief is an absolute contradiction to evidence. Look at the grass grow, look at how a forest regenerates after a fire, and look how animals survive in the wild. You don't see man having to plant seeds, trees, or run buckets of water to the wildlife. That is God taking care of His creations. When you do accept Him and make Him a part of your life, stop beating yourself up from your past. Forgive yourself, just like you do others. Compassionately recognize the frailty of another and realize that everything you do makes an enormous impact. Even the small choices are truly not small at all. With acceptance, let go, let God, and understand that the gift of waking up each morning is an act of God's divine plan for life."

– **Charles Moorer**

3

*I revealed myself to those who
did not ask for me;
I was found by those who
did not seek me*

(Isaiah 65:1)

Philosophically, God is always trying to get our attention in every circumstance. He does not force or push Himself into anyone's life. Instead, He patiently waits for each one of us to respond and willingly receive Him.

Reflecting on this truth brought to mind the age-old call and answer game of "Knock Knock, Who's There" in which so many of us are quick to answer the illusory door when the knock presents itself. If we could be as swift in opening our door to a personal relationship with God as we are for a joke, only then would our faith, love, hope, and perseverance find new muscles. God is inviting us to draw close to the true purpose of our creation, which is to know Him.

Alicia Britt-Chole is a Christian, wife, mother, author, speaker, and mentor. Every thought, choice, and action centers on her relationship with God where trust is at its very core.

To truly understand the energy she permeates, close your eyes and imagine the smell of honeysuckles on a late summer afternoon. Just like this flower, her presence is modest, her approach is sweet, her wisdom is digestible, and her conviction is powerful. I personally knock on your door and invite you to connect and engage both your heart and mind to her wise words and counsel in this chapter, through her writings, DVDs, and speaking engagements. Many of Alicia's quotes were excerpted with permission from her book, "Finding an Unseen God: Reflections of a Former Atheist".

Growing up a treasured only child in a home filled with constant encouragement and unconditional love and acceptance, both her parents supported her in everything she learned, from ballet to golf. She wore braces, explored every hobby and interest that ignited her appeal, and attained a college education in preparation for law school.

With religious and non-religious viewpoints entwined at home, there was no religious order on a daily basis. Her parents respected where each other stood in their beliefs about God.

At her mother's guidance and father's encouragement, Alicia was exposed to church every Sunday for eight years. Whenever she and her family moved, which was an annual occasion; her mother faithfully found a parish to attend and always did her best to get Alicia there.

Her father, an atheist, always kept the environment about him as one of openness and invitation where nothing was ever off limits. In no way did he ever disrespect or discourage what her mother attempted to do and in no way did he ever attempt to sway Alicia away from faith. Regardless of his disbelief, he felt that religious instruction was valuable as it provided people a morale framework. Nothing ever humiliated her father. Alicia could ask or talk about whatever was in her heart because questions were respected. She credited her father for not just giving her the first glimpse of atheism, but for also giving her the first glimpse of the divine because he mirrored the attributes of God that Alicia eventually found so captivating.

Around the age of nine or 10, Alicia sat with her parents one night and announced that religious activity was a creation of man to help fill gaps in their lives, a lot like a play, and she definitely did not want to play a part in such a fictitious performance. Afterward, her dad sat quietly and her mother sat heartbroken.

In the beginning, atheism was all "emotionally benign" because it did not have either the force or the label as it did later on in her life. Her choice wasn't even a departure of sorts. It wasn't as though she had a relationship with God and then decided that He no longer existed. For her, she was walking from nothing into the certainty of nothing, and it was a sincere decision she made.

Much more mature and knowledgeable in her concluded assessment now, Alicia revealed how she came into her faith. As she spoke, I was reminded of God's knocking.

In the beginning, it was the slow process of new friends. In high school, she met two young ladies, Shawn and Christi. Alicia stated that their first encounter with one another seemed almost choreographed. Together, side by side, these girls walked up to Alicia and said, "Hi, I'm Shawn, I'm Christi, and we're Christians."

Alicia looked at them and replied, "Were you two hoping for a cookie or looking for some kind of reward? Keep your faith to yourself."

Little did Alicia know that Shawn and Christi were determined to be friends with her whether she liked it or not; and the truth is, the three of them are friends to this day.

Alicia never questioned her decision or entertained the possibility that she could be wrong as an atheist. The reason for her certainty: Alicia rationalized that the "peace" both Shawn and Christi retained could only be from the fruit of never knowing any pain and that one day "life would come crashing down on them" dissolving their belief. In the meantime, Alicia confessed that whenever she was around them, she enjoyed their peacefulness while she remained completely disconnected from the source these two girls encompassed.

In the course of their friendship, several things happened between Alicia and these girls that not only weakened Alicia's lack of faith, but deepened theirs.

Whenever conversations about God were the topic, Alicia's demeanor was always argumentative and angry. Eventually, Shawn reached a point of frustration not only with Alicia's rigidity, but with her own inability to answer some of the questions presented.

One day, Shawn said to Alicia, "Okay! Well, what about this? I was at a church service and there was a woman. I know her Alicia. It's not like she was a stranger walking in from the street. I know her and I knew that she had been really, really, really sick. The man who was preaching prayed for her, laid his hands on her, and right then and there, she was healed. She walked out healed! What do you say about that?"

Shawn had completely gone out on a limb when she spoke about the supernatural. It not only startled Alicia, it stunned her. Unable to give an explanation, Alicia didn't know what to do with this information. She knew Shawn well enough to know that she was not an idiot, she was not delusional, and she was not lying. She was an intelligent woman who had seen something and the "supernatural" astonished her.

Then, on June 26, 1983, Alicia's life, views, and beliefs were mercifully interrupted. Four months before her 18th birthday and six weeks before she was to go to college, Alicia went to Illinois to spend a few days with Susie, a friend since grade school.

A day or two before she was to travel, Susie's mom, Mrs. Sokol, phoned her. With enthusiasm she said, "Alicia, we are glad you are coming to visit. I wanted you to know that this summer when you come, you are going to meet Jesus."

Taken aback, Alicia's immediate thought was, "They're everywhere! These Christians are everywhere!" Politely and almost empathetically, Alicia replied, "Mrs. Sokol, there is no Jesus to meet."

Once in Illinois, Alicia agreed to attend church with the Sokol family. She knew that all she had to do was survive one hour without being rude or falling asleep. Dressed in her finest purple miniskirt, she made her way across the parking lot toward the church. Everyone within view stared at her. Initially perplexed, Alicia shrugged off their gazes with the logical contemplation, "It must be the purple." That notion was far from the truth. She later learned that Mrs. Sokol had requested prayers from the entire church congregation for the Pagan staying with her.

There she sat in a tiny broken church on one of its last Sunday services with a gathering of people mostly in their 80's and an out of tune organ. Alicia was not there to begin "a noble truth search nor was she there to find a God; she was there to get rid of a Christian."

As the organ played and everyone began to sing, "it" happened. The moment was incredible and undeniable. The experience was not an emotional worship, moving message, or anything she could turn her back on. She wasn't drunk, she wasn't high, and she wasn't in the pit of despair. It was as if God removed everything Alicia could have possibly used as an excuse to deny Him.

Her awareness of everyone and everything in the church faded instantly. What remained was "not a nothingness, but a Presence; a sure, full, and distinct Presence that gently flowed over and through her" with great power. Alicia described it to the likes of a waterfall pouring over top. It was dynamic, spirited, and vigorous yet, refreshing. She declared, "It broke chains off of my mind dislodging chunks of dirt from the fabric of my soul." It was God. He had interrupted her entire life on every layer. The encounter was completely holistic and "to deny His existence would mean she would have to deny her very own," and in that moment, she knew the name of this Presence as it radiated from her soul, Jesus.

Having faith in God involves trust, a quality heavily lacking in today's society, and many people have trouble grasping this idea. On this topic, Alicia said, "Although our society is becoming more spiritual, it doesn't mean we all know how to nurture our spiritual selves. Many of us go from waking up, to reading the newspaper, to hopping in the car, to going to work, to eating, to watching the game, and then back to sleep just to do it all over again the next day.

What can change this? Relationships. Relationships make us hunger, and if we develop a rapport with people who nurture truth into our soul, we quickly realize first and foremost "what" will last after the day, after the job, and after retirement. If we also developed the ability to pause – to stop the busyness of our everyday lives – we might start asking some questions."

Alicia also declared that in order for a person to become inspired or enlightened about God, the virtues of faith, belief, or philosophy must truly be able to make a difference in their generation and for the broken in body, mind, and spirit.

God is the "center" of Alicia's life and when she honors Him and His ways in all that she thinks, says, and does, that "center" strengthens. If we too could interpret our relationships and daily dealings with God at the center, not only would our faith strengthen, but our relationships would be healthier and we would find everything we need.

True prioritization has some value, but is limited. *God first, family second* ... the saying is, "lovely and linear, but not livable." Resisting God's ways in interacting with others creates a distance in Alicia's relationships with God and nothing is worth that.

Knowing that everyone has times of comfort and times of struggle, faith grants and restores Alicia with spiritual and emotional strength when personal struggles weigh in on her. She professed, "Pain opens the door to greater intimacy with God. In life's most painful moments, those painful spaces in our lives are often the thresholds in which God is inviting us to draw closer to Him."

Alicia's life has revealed that faith in Jesus is sustainable through seasons of deep pain. One time, while in college, she debated with a Muslim man on the topic of Christ. Alicia explained that while she won the debate, her lack of love lost this man's trust. Following the experience, she listened more, spoke less, and soon felt a great obligation to whomever she interacted with. Her conclusion, "that for every soul on the planet, God is the powerful magnet drawing us to Him no matter what the occasion. God created us from His Spirit and we are always being drawn to Him."

Has she ever had a moment in the midst of pain where she bumped up against anything that made her think, "Wait a minute?!" Yes. Have there been times where she was conscience of the drawing, conscience of her soul being pulled to God's origins? Yes. Was she ever aware of a Holy attraction during her days as an atheist? Yes and no. She stated, "On the surface, I was aware of a woman, Mrs. Sokol, who was too kind to yell at, who strongly believed in something that I considered a myth, and who constantly invited me to church.

"Under the surface, I acknowledge and see that the two years of "presence of Presence" in my friendship with Shawn and Christy gradually eroded some of the protective mechanisms I had placed around myself."

These people were gifts. Jesus working through their lives was an awakening for her. The truth is: she responded to a two-year-plus process that she now visibly sees when she looks back.

Some people worry that because of their strongholds and addictions, they cannot get close to God. They worry that they are not righteous enough. Alicia stated, "No one is perfect. We all bear the fingerprints of God and regardless of the choices we make, God longs for us to know Him."

Prayer is strategic in nurturing Alicia's relationship with God. She does not always go to Him with petitions of "give me, help me, rescue me, or heal me." Instead, she communes with Him through her own stillness, silence, and solitude because the truth is, not everything in life or on our mind is going to have an answer. She stated, "Silence doesn't negate talking it out and it doesn't negate the community."

Just like Alicia, it will probably take years to carve out a sanctuary in your soul where you meet with Him without noise from the outside or chatter within, but when it's achieved, "God – not the answers we seek – will become our soul's treasure." It will become clear that "faith is not our creation. It's His."

Words of Encouragement

"Attend to your soul and Jesus will show you the way."
— **Alicia Britt Chole**

4

Thou wilt keep him in perfect peace, whose mind is stayed on Thee, because he trusteth in Thee

(Isaiah 26:3)

Finding balance in this life can be a daunting task that can sometimes bring troubles, fears, and sadness. But, if you pay better attention to the world around you, you will realize and acknowledge that all things living came into existence only by God. As a reminder, you too were created and therefore you are no accident.

The oldest child of two and the only son in the Wells family, Scott and his sister grew up in a home where love, integrity, morals, and faith in Christ were at its center.

Scott graduated from Radford University in 1988 with a bachelor's degree in business administration and over the past 22 years he has been a sales representative and is now the vice president of United Lighting and Supply.

From the time he was young, Scott loved music so much that he wrote, played, and performed. This passion took him from playing in bars and nightclubs to church and religious venues. When God called, Scott answered.

Aside from this day job in lighting, he serves as the Director of Music with '2nd Thief Ministries' and he is the ISCO-Founder of a music group known as The Rectifier's. (You can learn more about their band and their music at *www.therectifiers.com*.)

Scott and his band members chose the name 'The Rectifiers' because God's abilities are much like the device itself. Just as the rectifier is able to convert several electrical paths into one direct path, God is able to convert anyone and everyone's life path toward one positive direction: Him. Each band member's life has been rectified by God and it is the occurrences that have put them together as musicians and brothers in Christ.

God revealed His existence, power, mercy, and grace quite a few times in Scott's life. No one, not even the most hardened cynic, will ever change Scott's faith because nothing can change the truth.

When Scott was 15 years old, he suffered from a life-threatening condition called Myocarditis, a viral infection of the heart that caused his heart to swell to the size of a football and caused many other life threatening complications to attack his body. Scott battled for his life.

Once at Children's Hospital, the medical staff informed his parents of two harsh realities. They were told that Scott might not make it through the night and if he survived, he would have permanent scarred heart tissue which would limit his physical mobility, forever.

His parents did everything within their power to obtain the best medical treatment for Scott. They even turned to their faith for comfort, hope, and a miracle. Their church pastor visited them at the hospital and joined them in prayer while Scott's grandmother summoned her entire church congregation into prayer from afar.

In the late night hours and alone, Scott's mother held a silent, private, and deep vigil outside his room. She asked God to spare her son's life and in exchange she would give Him hers, in life or in death, whichever God preferred. Unbeknownst to her, and anyone else for that matter, Scott's father also held his own vigil in another location. Just like his wife, he too petitioned God to take his existence, in life or in death, in exchange for Scott's.

Incredibly, Scott survived the night and a couple of days later, a startling, unexpected, and unusual encounter followed. A man, whom neither of Scott's parents knew, arrived at the hospital unannounced and sought Scott out. Fortunately, the hospital staff was familiar with him so they promptly escorted him to Scott's room to meet with him and his parents. The nurses enlightened Scott's parents to the man's reputation as a healer as they had witnessed many miracles come from him.

Within the week, all complications left Scott's body. The entire Wells family credit the mercy of God and power of prayer for this miracle. From that day forward, his parents willingly gave God complete leadership over their lives as promised in prayer. They have proven themselves as doers of The Word and not just listeners.

Despite this event, Scott balanced himself on a spiritual fence of faith on one side and the world on the other. He thought he had God and his beliefs all figured out and he thought that if he did his best to obey God's Commandments, he would earn his way into Heaven. Despite of all his best efforts, Scott had no real peace or joy in his life because he never truly measured up to the standpoints he set up for himself. It seemed that the harder he tried, the more hopeless his walk with God became. Soon, life experiences emotionally brought him to a place of lowliness.

With nowhere to turn, Scott turned to God and that was when he realized that in order for him, or anyone else for that matter, to be a successful believer, he must willingly be dependent upon the guidance and hand of God and not himself. This was when he handed his entire life over to God.

Scott has been married 17 years and counting to the love of his life, Terri. They have two bright and articulate children, Marshall and Victoria, whom they both constantly lead toward God.

Scott admitted that the deciding factors that initially lured him into a relationship with Terri were her looks, her body, and what she could do for him. The added fact that she was smart was a bonus. Beauty plus brains, what a package!

Nowadays, that influence in their relationship with one another is God. He is at the center of their individual lives and their marriage. They both declared that keeping His commands are their priorities and this results in a constant pouring of blessings onto them and their family.

Scott spoke about his wife and how the gift of having her by his side helped him build his faith. He said, "Certainly, for those of us who God has joined together as one flesh, there isn't much outside our relationship with Jesus Christ that can build faith like the help and encouragement of a faithful wife and what she brings to it."

Throughout the Bible, there is a constant abiding structure of trust, loyalty, commitment, and respect to those who abide to God's Word. As you read the Scriptures below, sense them and contemplate how you and your relationships could improve. These attributes are within Scott's marriage:

"Then the LORD God said, 'It is not good for the man to be alone; I will make him a helper suitable for him." (Genesis 2:18)

"For this reason a man shall leave his father and his mother, and be joined to his wife; and they shall become one flesh." (Genesis 2:24)

"If it is disagreeable in your sight to serve the LORD, choose for yourselves today whom you will serve: whether the gods which your fathers served which were beyond the River, or the gods of the Amorites in whose land you are living; but as for me and my house, we will serve the LORD." (Joshua 24:15)

"Trust in the LORD with all your heart and do not lean on your own understanding. In all your ways acknowledge Him, and He will make your paths straight." (Proverbs 3:5-6)

"Hatred stirs up strife, but love covers all transgressions." (Proverbs 10:12)

"Let all bitterness and wrath and anger and brawling and slander be put away from you, along with all malice. Be kind to one another, tenderhearted, and forgiving each other just as God in Christ also has forgiven you." (Ephesians 4:31-32)

"Submit to one another out of reverence for Christ. Wives, be subject to your own husbands, as to the Lord. For the husband is the head of the wife as Christ also is the head of the church, He Himself being the Savior of the body. But as the church is subject to Christ, so also the wives ought to be to their husbands in everything. Husbands, love your wives, just as Christ also loved the church and gave Himself up for her, so that He might sanctify her, having cleansed her by the washing of water with the word, that He might present to Himself the church in all her glory, having no spot or wrinkle or any such thing; but that she would be holy and blameless. So husbands ought also to love their own wives as their own bodies. He who loves his own wife loves himself; for no one ever hated his own flesh, but nourishes and cherishes it, just as

Christ also does the church, because we are members of His body. For this reason a man shall leave his father and mother and shall be joined to his wife, and the two shall become one flesh. This mystery is great; but I am speaking with reference to Christ and the church. Nevertheless, each individual among you also is to love his own wife as himself, and the wife must see to it that she respects her husband." (Ephesians 5:21-33)

"You husbands likewise, live with your wives in an understanding way, as with a weaker vessel, since she is a woman; and grant her honor as a fellow heir of the grace of life, so that your prayers may not be hindered." (1 Peter 3:7)

These passages all speak the sense of loyalty that exists in a marriage when Christ is at the center.

Is every day blissful in the home and marriage of Scott and Terri Wells? No; however, Scott does not abuse his role as the "head of household." He does not belittle, control, or talk down to Terri while expecting her to take whatever he dishes out or wants. Whereas, Terri never blindly follows behind Scott's leading, but she does not disrespect him or desire to control and change him either.

What makes their marriage work is this: They take each other's needs, feelings, and desires into themselves much the same way Jesus asks of us, "Abide in me and I will abide in you ..." (John 15:4). Scott is in Terri and Terri is in Scott. They pledge themselves to the plans and priorities of God.

Another God and Scott encounter was witnessed several years back. Terri said, "I witnessed a total transformation in Scott at a memorial service held for families who had lost a child or children. He was supposed to sing and play a song that he had written, but he lost his voice due to overuse just hours before he was to perform.

"As the day progressed, Scott started to panic and in total desperation he gargled with salt water and ate lozenges by the handful. By the time of the service, he literally had no voice – nothing. Neither one of us had any idea about what to do. Then, he walked into the adjacent choir room to have some quiet time alone. I don't remember how long he was in there, but when Scott emerged and walked back into the sanctuary, I noticed a visible change in him. Right away, I knew that a miracle had just happened almost before my eyes. He was completely healed and able to perform.

"Afterward, when we were alone, I asked him what happened. Scott told me that he laid the problem down in total surrender to God and asked for His Will to be done. It was in that very moment that an extreme sense of calm and peace came over him. He felt God's Spirit enter his body."

This is the example of "total surrender." In that time of personal need, when his voice had disappeared and he felt broken in hope, Scott prayed and handed the circumstance over to God to see what He could do with it. As far as Scott was concerned, he had nothing to lose because he had nowhere else to turn. In turn, Scott gave God greater leadership of his life.

One might think Scott tested faith in that moment, but it was faith that tested Scott. Healing took place because of one reason and one reason only: the hand of God was upon him. Scott stated, "Faith has taught me to look outside of my own abilities and power. Without Jesus Christ, we are nothing but dust.

This account is a testimony to the power of Christ! By His Spirit within us, we are able to exercise the same faith that Jesus teaches about in the Bible. "And they (God's people) overcame him (Satan) by the blood of the Lamb (Jesus) and by the word (faith) of their testimony..." (Revelation 12:11). This Scripture clearly points to the power of our words in overcoming the enemy. All glory goes to God for performing miracles proving that the Love of God can be a witness through a person."

Although faith does not keep a Christian immune to the ups and downs of life, it does keep their waters calm when the storms of adversity roll in. A relationship with God provides - strength, patience, perseverance, and love – in how you will react to situations compared.

Scott said, "A Christian is one who comes to know that their life is not their own. They put to death their old life and desire to live out the ministry of Jesus Christ through the new life He gives them. A Christian loves everyone, all who they come across in spirit and in truth."

For those of you who struggle with this view on faith, but would like to embrace it, Scott advised that the first thing you must do is figuratively die. Once you deny yourself and yield to God's will, Heaven here on earth will be discovered. Scott declared, "If you want to live with God in Heaven, you better start living with God here on earth, in your life and in your heart!"

The same Creator that made the earth, this universe, and all the "matter" that has ever been made, also made you. You will meet Him face to face one day depending upon your willingness to let go of your grip on this life. Scott cautioned, "Release the control you think you have over your own destiny and believe in His Son, Jesus, because you will meet him one day as either your Father or your Judge."

In other words, give up the independence you have demanded from God. Stop trying to do things your way. Deny your worldly and ungodly cravings such as sexual immorality, dirty mindedness, evil thoughts, and lusts for other people's goods. Allow yourself to hear that still small voice inside you which will guide you into His plan. Focus on Jesus through prayer, meditate on His sufferings, and read God's written Word.

God's Word tells us that the battle is the Lord's, His burden is light, His yoke is easy, and the Word repeatedly points to the fact that true Christian fellowship can only exist among believers. We should hold each other accountable for shortcomings and strongholds while constantly teaching and admonishing each other. This sharpens and encourages our daily walk.

Scott stated, "When you turn to God and to the inspiration of His Word in the Bible while amidst your storms is when He truly becomes alive and ministers to you. His Spirit will guide you into truth and honor. Do these two things while in a constant state of awareness to Jesus' sacrifice and your character will become exactly what Christ said it should be."

The incident that reinforced this belief occurred in Scott's early stages of faith. Regardless of how much he loved God, he occasionally harbored resentment towards those who either hurt him, a family member, or a personal friend. One day, God revealed to him that this "attitude" was not a Christ-like quality and that He wanted him to be rid of it. Not sure how to go about this, Scott's thoughts were soon consumed with the image of Jesus' suffering and pleas when crucified at Calvary. As He hung beaten, disrobed, and condemned by the world, Jesus remained filled with unconditional love and asked God to forgive the people who had put Him there. These thoughts prompted him to conclude, "Who am I to judge, condemn, and be angry with someone?" With exuberance Scott continued, "Can you imagine the peace that comes from being able to accept, forgive and love everyone you meet regardless of how they treat you?"

With God this is possible! You will start to see everyone as God sees them: made in His own image and created to glorify Him in this life when they invite Him into their heart. Scott made the choice to forgive everyone, no matter what they said or did and since then, he has lived a more peace-filled life and remains focused more on the needs of others than his own. He asserted that God's love is a tangible love that can be felt and recognized. God's answers and guidance that flow into Scott's thoughts, choices, and actions are all centered from a place of love; not lust, greed, or selfishness.

God is and has always been the "Supreme Being" and He exists in three individuals: Father, Son, and Holy Spirit. Together, they are One. Because God created all things, He is the very essence of love. He alone is the author and finisher of our lives and faith. Only through God's power can we truly have faith at all.

The presence of Presence has blessed Scott and his family beyond measure. Not only has his faith been disciplined by obedience, it has been nurtured. Most recently, it was nurtured through the witnessing of two friends who came into a relationship with Christ the very night their child died.

Through Jesus Christ, Scott sees the worlds' riches and trappings for what they really are – nothing. As a young man, he thought he had life all figured out. He tried to do the right things, enjoy his life, and appreciate the world around him. He even made some good friendships along the way, but there was one problem through all of it: his motives. They weren't exactly honorable, not the way he knows God wants them to be.

He admitted to having moments in his earlier life where his choice to be kind was to feel good within him, gain something materialistic, or receive recognition. All these things were about stroking his ego, not pleasing God. Scott encouraged, "Reflect on the true motives behinds your actions and remember this worldly and Godly truth: While the things of this world can bring pleasure, they are temporary and never last. As for friendships, they too come and go. Quite often, we let our friends down and they let us down because we set each other up with personal expectations. Stop that! You're just asking for disappointment."

So, how can you come to know God and have any faith in Him if you refrain from speaking directly to Him? Even by the world's standards, how can you trust another person if you never speak to them? The best communication is prayer. Trust perfected is prayer perfected. Trust looks to receive the thing asked for and gets it. Trust is not a belief that God can or will bless, but that He 'does' bless here and now. Trust always operates in the present tense which produces hope and hope looks toward the future. Trust looks to the present. Hope expects. Trust possesses. Trust receives what prayer acquires. So, what prayer needs at all times is abiding and abundant trust.

God wants to have a trusting relationship with us. We were not created just so we could be in Heaven with Him. We were created to find Him, know Him, trust Him, obey Him, and love Him while living life. We were created to live with Him in relation as we would with our own physical parents. God will bear the burdens of your life if you let Him.

Besides prayer, the spiritual practices that further nurture our faith are: meditation (sitting in silence), Bible study, and breaking bread with others. God tells us to gather together, study the Holy Scriptures, and apply the understanding of His written Word into our lives. Through the power of prayer, faith is exercised and mountains of adversity are moved.

To fully experience God, Scott takes time away from his family and phone calls to quiet his mind and heart. By eliminating worries, concerns, and thoughts, he rests in the quiet communion of His holy Presence.

God is the first person he speaks to in the morning and the last person he speaks to at night along with periodic conversations with Him throughout his day. He seeks Him and sees Him in all things, small and large – from when he dresses for the day to how he responds to every person he encounters throughout the day. After giving thanks for all things, Scott asks God to guide him with His Holy Spirit. This is when God's presence is felt.

We have all been gifted by God for the purpose of giving. All God wants each of us to do is to glorify Him with praise and thankfulness and to give to others worthy of His making and calling.

Scott encouraged us to find the gift that we are truly passionate about. Whether your gift is cooking, babysitting, building, drawing, dancing, or anything else, exercise and use it for the good of others. This is the way to honor God and point others to the mercy and grace of Jesus.

When Scott reached the point in his life where he recognized God's desire for him to live out His ministry through and beyond music, Scott claimed that the calling was liberating. No longer did he struggle with his flesh, ego, or God's will for him. Again, Scott affirmed, "Once you believe, rest, and allow the Holy Spirit to work in your life, mountains of adversity move.

"The Spirit of God will lead you into all truth and above all things, love. Love your friends, all people, and especially your enemies, which is the most difficult. When you do these, you prove to God and the world how much you love Him."

Words of Encouragement

"Believing God and believing in God are two different things. In this life you will have struggles and you will experience let downs especially from those near and dear to you, but if you surrender everything to Jesus, life will take on a whole new perspective.

"The span of this life pales in comparison to eternity. We were all born and we are all going to die. While you don't have any control over your impending death, you do have control over where your soul will spend eternity. Are the lusts of this world really worth the damage you cause others in life or your eternal destination? Are you sure that you want to gamble that? It doesn't matter how good a person you are or how much kindness you show to others. That does not guarantee you a seat in Heaven. God tells us that all have fallen short of the glory of God

"You can have Heaven on earth now and you can know God now. The love you will have for Him and from Him will spill into your relationships here on earth. Through Him, there is an abundance of peace and trust that you cannot attain on your own. If you keep depending on yourself, you are going to keep failing. Aren't you tired? Seek Him, invite Him, discover Him, and rest with Him. God made you and He loves you. He knew you before He knitted you in your mother's womb. He wants all of you. Come to him and trust Him at His Word and your soul will never go hungry or thirsty. This He promises and I testify to this."

– **Scott Wells**

5

As in mind, so in manifestation

H.P. Blavatsky once said, "Spiritual and divine powers lie dormant in every human being and the wider the sweep of his spiritual vision, the mightier will be the God within."

Many people either deny the very existence of God or believe that a person's imagination is what serves them in both their creativity and faith. These people are those who are blind to God's Spirit and its manifestations that others are wise and connected to.

Jenny Wild, the middle child of three girls, was born in South Bend, Indiana and was raised in Mt. Clemens, Michigan. Regardless of the degree in different personalities she and her sisters possessed, they have always gotten along with each other and remain lovingly close to one another today. In fact, Jenny referred to her sisters as her best friends.

A cheerleader and a member of a three-girl folk singing group called, The Wilders, Jenny was socially active in and out of high school.

Her parents kept life at home structured and disciplined with gentleness. Many neighborhood kids considered Jenny's family as their "home away from home" because of her parent's approach, respect, actions, and life coaching techniques. Her parents encouraged strong morals, honesty, self-respect, and kindness to others, as well as to themselves.

Her father, a gentle man and true role model of leadership enjoyed life, his wife, and his daughters. His ongoing interest in their lives kept him young at heart and made their time spent together never a dull moment. Among Jenny's favorite memories are the times when he would fix a huge bowl of popcorn covered in parmesan cheese and then would sit around with all of them as they ate, talked, and laughed.

Her mother, a loving, strong, and no-nonsense woman worked as a nurse. She was loved and trusted by everyone. She was the adult that the neighborhood kids went to for respected conversations and straight up answers as most subjects were never off limits with her. Her mother respected a child's youth and individuality and in return, the kids loved her.

As for religion, Jenny was raised Catholic and her faith in Jesus Christ was firmly established through Catholic teachings and practices. Jenny stated that when she was a young girl, she wanted to be a nun, but that aspiration was short-lived when she later realized that there were many other options in life open to her – and boys were one of them.

Today, she refrains from claiming herself to be of any particular denomination; however, she does declare herself and everyone else for that matter, as a child of God. We are all brothers and sisters in Christ.

Two significant accounts during her college days, one analytical and the other metaphysical, solidified Jenny's belief in God.

Analytically, she explored several religions and denominations along with their beliefs and practices. Metaphysically, she explored Divine Science, an abstract, systematic, and spiritual teaching of the Bible through interpretation, meditation, application, and prayer all combined with the power of a person's mind.

The Divine Science class enforced her belief that a Higher Power is at the forefront of life every day. God is the spirit in all living things and we are all connected through Him for we are His creation.

Metaphysically, Jenny personally experienced the presence, power, and embrace of the Holy Spirit. As she recalled and shared the event, her demeanor quickly radiated immense reverence for God. Softly, she said, "When I was in college, I attended church every Sunday just as I did growing up. During one particular service, the Holy Spirit came into the room and upon me. I can't recall how long it lasted, but the experience wasn't scary or uncomfortable. What I saw was light, what I heard was singing, and what I felt was a presence emanating an intense amount of peace, joy, and love like I had never felt before or after. The Presence was beautiful, opulent, and sovereign."

God entwined with the teachings of Divine Science anchored Jenny's belief and knowledge that our experiences can lead our mind and drive the approach of how we live each day and react to situations. Without argument, she comprehends how we can view a day simply as a day that "just happens" to us thereby creating an "Oh, poor me" attitude with us. That mind-set will only cause us to seek pity from others and can easily lead to a cycle of reckless thinking where our attitudes drift into a state of anger and resentment about life, people, and God.

Jenny stated, "The truth is, we are solely responsible for our own misery and our own hell a majority of the time. If we really pay attention to our surroundings, we will see a lot of this negative behavior reinforced in the media. We witness people in shows and in commercials who exemplify selfishness. We may not realize it, but we are setting up the stage and we are creating a generation of consumers, not citizens...for what, money? This perspective is frightening. We need to change our minds and we need to change our thinking."

Faith is the power that changes a person's mind and heart. Faith helps us to replace fear, worry, doubt, and hate with love. Faith gives hope that all things work out for the good and faith produces the power of right thinking releasing into expression health, abundance, peace, and power into each individual life.

Saying positive affirmations on a continual basis is a good way to help reprogram your mind, but nothing is more powerful than a personal relationship with Christ. Through and with God, you will better examine your thinking so that you may understand the reasons for your discomfort. By leaning on Him, you will find strength to accept, understand, and know how to get through your predicaments no matter how good or bad they are.

Jenny shared a "God moment" encounter in her life that stays near and dear to her heart. As you read, you will have the urge to debunk her explanation, but I encourage you to pay attention because the only explanation is a divine one.

Years ago, Jenny was caught in a terrible snowstorm. It was late at night and the streets were empty. She was stuck in her car in a deserted parking lot and as you can imagine, she was feeling anxious, desperate, and scared. From out of nowhere, three young men suddenly appeared and pushed her car out of the parking lot. Once she attained traction, Jenny put her car in park and got out to thank them, but the men could not be found. In fact, their footprints could not be traced. Jenny looked everywhere to see which direction they might have walked off to, but the only remnants in the snow were her own boot prints and car tires. The three men were guardian angels sent to help her.

As a business owner, Jenny has experienced the less than joyful encounter of people who purposely set out to destroy and dismantle her business. Rather than losing her sense of peace and composure, she emotionally placed every situation at the feet of Jesus, raised her hands up in the air as a gesture of letting go and asked God for guidance. In every circumstance, God steered her through and around the difficulties.

Then, there was the time she bid on a job. She and her team of colleagues had to prepare, deliver, and submit a proposal in a very fast turnaround time. The pressure for time with this sensitive material meant many late night hours for everyone. When the task was completed and submitted, Jenny was thrilled for beating the appointed deadline. The next day, Jenny was notified that the project in its entirety had been rescinded. Tired, disappointed, and no plan B up her sleeve, she fell into an emotional slump. At the same time this happened, she and her partner were headed out for a one week retreat of rest and relaxation in the beautiful and tranquil state of Maine. While there, she spent several days sitting around in a foggy state of gloom.

One morning, she repositioned her intellect as an observer of herself and her surroundings. She asked herself, "Why were you so connected to the project? Why did you find its failure so hurtful? Was it the money? Was it being able to take care of people? Was it about being productive or a job well done?" Then, she remembered what she had forgotten, "Everything happens for a reason, reasons that are beyond our control and when we finally let go, something good always comes from it."

Jenny encouraged, "All of us need to emotionally let go of unsettling situations no matter what they may be. When we go to a place of peace, a place of no worries, and a place of centeredness on God and give

Him all our concerns, that is when our minds are set free and everything that God has in store for us begins to transpire."

Things of this world are no longer her center of life. God and all His wondrous works are. She strives to live in the "here and now" knowing that her spiritual journey in itself has been and is a blessing. God is her source, and she is the individualized expression of Him as we all are.

In the book of Matthew, not only is the life and ministry of Jesus revealed, but so are the fulfillment of prophecies in the Old Testament along with several miraculous healings that substantiate Jesus as who He is claimed to be.

"...According to your faith, will it be done to you..." (Matthew 9:29). Think and contemplate how this Scripture relates to your own life as I share manifestations in Jenny's life that validate this scripture.

Jenny stated that her horse, home, and current work schedule are all physical manifestations of this scripture and its phenomenon. In sincerity and a sense of adventure, she develops a "bucket list" every year which details all the things she would like to accomplish. It is amazing to her that once she writes what she wants on paper; most of the things listed seem to materialize at warp speed. She said, "I wanted to spend time with my horse, I wanted a home in a particular town, I wanted to continue my yoga, I wanted the freedom to read spiritual literature that evolves my soul, and I wanted to enjoy all of it. It's here. I have it! As a matter of fact, I was going through some boxes a while back and came upon a slip of paper with notations that I had written two years ago. The paper read, 'Perfect House: three fireplaces, large deck, two nice bedrooms, a nice office, and all the amenities.' Everything that I had written on that list is here for me today."

Everything in life has its place. "Faith puts energy into desires and God always has a much better plan than anyone of us could ever imagine," she explained.

Jenny's relationship with God has made a significant impact in her relationship with others, especially her partner. She stated, "Our home is supposed to be a place of refuge where we and everyone within it find love, safety, support, and encouragement. While these assets are great expectations and intentions, the reality is a good majority of us don't always provide or feel these with one another.

"You will go through good times and bad times with one another. There will be times when your partner will drive you crazy and you might not even like them, but if you can take a step back from the situation that is irritating you and remember why you fell in love with that person in the first place, you will realize that the love is truly never gone."

We need to stop focusing on the flaws and shortcomings of another – especially after minor incidents – and communicate about the big and little things without yelling at one another. She declared, "Being the best of friends is the key to a healthy, long, and loving relationship. Being best friends involves being able to sit down and tell your partner how you're feeling if something is bothering you and of course being able to listen if your partner comes to you with comments or expressions of concern, care, and remorse.

"Couples don't necessarily need to be equally yoked on everything. If that were the case, can you imagine how boring and predictable your relationship would be? The qualities that need to be equally yoked are your ethics, integrity, values, and beliefs. These are imperative to enhance, strengthen, and survive any relationship, especially your intimate one."

We are meant to be with certain people at certain times in our lives. There are reasons for each person that comes to us even though we may not realize what those reasons are. Learn something from each new person. If your partner is abusing you or cheating on you, Jenny encouraged, "Leave that relationship!" However, if their worst offense is that they leave the toilet seat up or burp at the table, get over it.

Words of Encouragement

"People have a tendency to learn for themselves and learn through the actions of others. Expect more of yourself than others and live in a manner that others would want to emulate. The reputation of your character is far more important than what and how much you possess."

— **Jenny Wild**

6

God is within

An ancient prophet once said, "There is no worse blind man than the one who doesn't want to see; no worse deaf man than the one who doesn't want to hear; and no worse mad man than the one who doesn't want to understand." Anyone who has ever wrestled with doubt or moments of disbelief understands how during these times a person can become a rule and a standard to himself. Kenny witnessed this metaphoric madness while keeping his feet planted in something far greater than himself while growing up.

Having lived in Ventura, California his entire life, Kenny Wise expressed a tone of gratitude for having the luxurious benefit of a beach on one side and mountains on the other. As a child, he played softball, rode bicycles, rode skateboards, created artwork, and built forts. At the age of nine, he acquired the very unique hobby of raising rabbits of all breeds and continued this hobby until he was in his mid-20s. He credited this hobby to his early sense of maturity and dependability due to the responsibility it required. The business of rabbits kept him too busy to get into any trouble.

Kenny's mom, a spiritual woman, has always been a positive influence in his life. He credits her for keeping his creative juices flowing through art and illuminating discussions about life. Whenever Kenny experienced less than desirable circumstances, his mother encouraged him to speak his mind while she remained lovingly supportive. After hearing him out, she would then place her "twist" on things. The "twist" always impelled Kenny to take an emotional step back and weigh up a situation from the other person's perspective. Without fail, his conclusion, choice of words, and choice of actions would then be approached peacefully and sensibly compared to what he initially felt.

For instance, when Kenny was in sixth grade, he had just gotten a new Bane Skateboard with Chicago trucks and Cadillac wheels. On a shopping errand with his mother and older brother, Kenny remained outside of the stores and rode his skateboard. As he skated around, some older kids approached him. They wanted to ride it or at least, stand on it to test its flex. Kenny told the boys no, but their requests persisted. Finally, Kenny agreed and when he gave them that lead way, the kids took off with his skateboard.

Shocked, upset, and angry, Kenny shared his frustration about the situation to his mother and after he finished, she put her "twist" on it. Compassionate to his emotional state, she gently enlightened him to the sad fact that there are some people in the world of all ages who live unhappy lives and whose homes are filled with both anger and cruelty which make them behave exactly the way those kids did. As he contemplated the scenario as a true possibility, his heart and emotions softened to sympathy and compassion. He found peace amidst his anguish.

As for Kenny's father, he was a loving dad who occasionally took his family on excursions like camping and ski trips. With enthusiasm, he taught his children that they were capable of achieving whatever they set their minds to. His moments of family centeredness were genuine; however, something within him kept his eyes, heart, and mind intensely drawn to the world. Most of the time, he lived a very tempestuous, limitless, and selfish life. So much so, that he left his wife and family.

Years later, Kenny and his siblings all agreed that their father's departure was for the best. In its entirety, his childhood was a blessing because there was always food on the table, a great house to live in, a father's zeal, and a mother's love. With truth and empathy, he said, "Most of us don't get away with a perfect childhood and I believe that we are all here to learn. As parents, we do the best we can with the tools we've been taught."

The lessons learned about relationships when harnessed to faith are many. Kenny stated, "Knowing and embracing God into your life brings nothing but rewards with it; especially, a couple in unification together. When a couple has the same values, neither one of them hold false ideas and expectations over the other. They are free to be themselves and accept one another as is.

"God is an experience that forever changed my life with richness in how I see my spouse, kids, family, friends, people, circumstances, and nature. We all have the freedom to choose and because we act out of either love or fear in all our thoughts and choices, it's the fearful ones that bring suffering for ourselves, our partner, and our family. If we honor God, we automatically honor one another and a trusting relationship with Him manifests a trusting relationship with others."

God lives within all of us. He is the truth of who we are while we are having this experience called life that we share. While it is okay to hate another person's actions, we should not hate the person. We are to love their soul and accept them for who they are. He said, "I know that God appears as an illusion, but the truth is, God is all about love and we are too or at least, we are supposed to be."

Kenny shared his belief that the generations to come are better equipped for life than we have been and they will be able to do things a lot differently – maybe even to break the chain of worldly bondage that runs in and ruins many families.

The church Kenny's family attended when he was a child was significantly fundamental. The environment was a very God-fearing one that Kenny never intellectually connected with. The fear of living life on the judgment side of God never made sense to him. He believes in a loving and forgiving God – a God whose arms are wide open and waiting for each of us to embrace Him. Kenny's poise, presence, and characteristic are very connected to the life of Jesus.

He established a loving and trusting relationship with Christ through a meditation class. He learned to open up any narrowed thinking to someone far beyond anything tangible without being scientifically proven or authenticated by touch or sight. Kenny stated, "If you can get out of your own way and set your ego and fear aside, God's Spirit will flow into and through you. You will recognize Him because everything that comes from Him comes through with pure love.

"Faithfulness comes from within, grace flows from that space, and the gifts are the miracles that are always around us. It's our birthright and it's waiting for us to receive it."

Kenny connects with God five nights a week or more. The practice of meditation has blessed him with restful nights and the best dreams because God's Spirit flows freely through him. In fact, his dreams have brought answers to questions that were perhaps only a thought earlier in the day. In addition, when adversity strikes him, like it does all of us, meditation has taught Kenny to remain in a place of emotional peace and balance. As for God moments in his life, Kenny recalled three events.

When his wife, Heather, was pregnant with their son Josh, she had started passing a lot of blood. She was diagnosed with a tumor connected to the placenta. In quest of God's grace, mercy, and healing, Kenny got his daughter and a congregation of friends together for prayer and "laying of the hands" on both Heather and the baby. Two weeks later, the tumor disappeared and from that moment on, his wife never experienced any other complications.

The second incident occurred about 30 years ago. Kenny and a friend hiked up one of the many mountains in California when they came across a location that overlooked the valleys below all the way to the ocean. It was a beautiful and tranquil location, and Kenny fell in love with it. He visited the location quite often and while there, he would sit, aspire, and lay out their dream home with rocks as if it were already in physical form.

As time passed, Kenny's hold onto that dream eventually passed too, but the power of his intentions back then sure didn't. Twenty years later, a piece of mountain property was offered to Kenny and his wife. Once at the site, they both quickly realized they were standing two ridges to the east from where he had originally laid out his rocks. They bought the property, worked on it for over 10 years, and recently finished their dream home.

The third and most recent experience involved some work at his art studio, work he does aside from his day job.

A friend of Kenny's delivered him some very delicate Internment Camp posters that were once used as street advertisements during the 1940s. He asked Kenny to frame them as a gift for another friend whose grandmother would promptly remove and hide them in her attic whenever they were placed near her home back then. Then, just as he does with all pieces of work that come for his professional touch, Kenny placed the posters in cardboard and then inside one of his protective archival drawers.

About a month later, Kenny went to retrieve the posters to begin work, but he couldn't find them. He searched his studio several times and needless to say, he was weak in the knees and a nervous wreck for having lost them.

That night, while in meditation, Kenny was reminded of two very important things he did not do to find the posters. He did not give the situation over to God nor did he ask God for help so, before heading off to sleep, he prayed, "Okay God. It's all yours. Take it." As he slept, Kenny had three dreams. While each dream reconciled the posters to his hands, each dream also pointed him to different locations. Not sure which path to follow, he knew he had to search all three places.

After getting ready for his day the very next morning, Kenny phoned his friend to inform him that not only had he lost the posters, but that God had also given him three visions of where to look for them. He promised Steve that once he got back to his studio that evening, he would follow up on those visions and find them. Confident in Kenny's proclamation, Steve remained calm and trustful.

That evening, while back at home, Kenny sat down at his piano, played, and began to unwind from his day. While he played, he remembered his conversation with Steve and remembered his dreams. Immediately, he went to his studio and began the search. As envisioned, he looked on top of the refrigerator, but they weren't there. Next, he looked behind the mat cutter, but they weren't there either.

Then, he walked over to the archival drawer where he had originally placed them, pulled it open, reached his hand all the way into the backside behind it, and sure enough, he felt some cardboard. When he pulled it out, there they were. He phoned his friend, told him that he found them, and began the framing.

Regardless if moments feel good or bad, Kenny views them as a blessing. God is undoubtedly behind each and every experience.

Words of Encouragement

"God lives within all of us and He is the truth of who we are while we are having this human experience that we all share. Let us then allow God to walk in front of us so that we may not only move through this life with each other in love, but with personal knowledge that God lives within."

– **Kenny Wise**

7

Each one should use whatever gift he has received to serve others, faithfully administering God's grace in its various forms
(1 Peter 4:10)

~~~~~~

As children of God, we are called to be the Lord's hands and feet availing ourselves to the gifts bestowed upon us in serving one another. The rewards of yielding ourselves with the pure motive of pleasing God for the good of others consists of feeling and attaining assurance in His strength, perseverance, and peace in every aspect of our lives. This assurance keeps both our lives and our minds in a state of harmonious peace dispensing nothing but faithfulness, respect, self-control, compassion, perseverance, and love.

Wilton Ward is 83 years young and is the second oldest of six children all of whom were born and raised in a strong Christian home on a farm in North Carolina. He is a dedicated husband, loving father, trusted neighbor, and dependable friend.

Aware that not everyone has had an upbringing like his, Wilton stated that he was born a Christian. He can't recall a time when his parents did not embrace the Bible as the handbook to life. They were obedient to The Word, their actions spoke volumes in belief, trust, obedience, and dependency in God when they too had to endure struggle, and he witnessed them stand firm and stand strong upon that rock of God, which we are all called upon to do. They definitely practiced what they preached.

His upbringing embedded an exceptional relationship between him and God, one of complete acceptance and trust that Wilton has never questioned or wavered away from. He does not shout, brag, or claim himself to be holier than anyone else, but when approached on the topic of God, Jesus Christ, and the Holy Spirit, he whispers, confesses, professes, admits, believes, and shares God's good grace. Wilton is soft-spoken with a grandfather quality that gently sets you at ease just being in his presence.

Practicality concludes that his gift in life was agriculture, but exemplification concludes that his gift in life has been and is serving. He has educated others in agriculture as a source of income or food for their families; and as a federal worker, he has provided federal credit assistance to low income farmers, and housing for low rural residents which included water, sewer, and other community services.

God is in everyone and everything. He is behind every circumstance even after Satan has wreaked havoc, pain, and suffering in the lives of His children. God brings something good out of our something bad, and He blesses those who are obedient. As we talked, he shared some personal incidents that encouraged this truth.

Wilton's older and late brother, Harold, experienced some marital troubles. As a modest man who lived a very modest lifestyle, Harold never spoke to anyone about his personal affairs much less his feelings. He kept to himself.

One day, Harold did something out of the ordinary. He bought himself a brand new dress suit and visited their sister, Vermell, in the middle of the day at her place of work. The first thing Vermell noticed was his new attire. He looked very dapper. Harold informed her that he was getting ready to leave for a business trip and the length of his trip was going to be a rather long one; in fact, there was high probability he would not be coming back at all. Sweet naïve Vermell never contemplated the depth or the real significance behind his message. As he went on, he told her where to locate his personal papers if she needed them and he made her promise to look after his kids. Lovingly, she promised and hugged him farewell.

Later that afternoon, Vermell, Wilton, and the rest of their family learned that Harold had gone home and had taken his own life. Almost in disbelief that it ever took place, Wilton said, "There were three things simultaneously out of character of Harold that day. Three things that Vermell and everyone else around him never pieced together as a cry for help."

The loss of his brother was not due to intentional neglect from Wilton or any other family member. However, the incident deeply shaped Wilton's consciousness and heart to be more aware of others needs and the importance of giving.

During a road trip home several years ago, Wilton pulled into a rest stop and was abruptly approached by a man unkempt and desperate in appearance. Wilton learned that the man was traveling to New York for a family emergency when his tire went flat and then later, his spare went flat.

Without a second thought, Wilton escorted the man to the next town to find a tire shop. They were successful in their search and the man got a really good deal on the price. Back at the rest stop, Wilton's mode of service continued. He did what he could to help replace both tires.

Astounded at the details of this encounter, some of Wilton's friend told him that he had put his life in danger by helping a stranger, but he knows different. Besides, the demonstration of gratitude expressed by the man in return for such benevolence was immense and something Wilton has never forgotten. He stressed, "It's what God would have done and honestly, I can only hope that someone would do that for me if I was ever in a similar situation."

Regardless of this event and other wonderful God-moments throughout his life, abundant substantiation of God's sovereignty was revealed in 1984 when his wife, Peggy, was diagnosed with breast cancer.

Despite how knowledgeable the doctors were, they told her that she had no choice but to have a mastectomy to save her life. As Peggy lay in recovery, the doctor informed Wilton that during the operation he was encouraged to look deeper, beyond the location of surgery as originally planned. When he followed this inner nudging, he discovered another tumor that had been undetected by all the previous ct scans. It was removed right away.

Stunned, both Wilton and the doctor knew that if he had not acted upon this premonition, the tumor would have remained and Peggy would have survived only two more years.

Wilton stated, "It's times like these that you know God is with you in all phases of your life. When the gifts He has created within are used for the greater good of another. While these experiences may not mean much to someone else, they mean a great deal to me.

"I know without a doubt that when a person of faith, religion, belief, or even disbelief truly pays attention, they see and experience the difference in the lives of God-filled believers. God is the spirit that moves for the good in the lives of people. Accepting this truth will transform lives for the better and make the world an improved place to live."

As mentioned before, no one's life is without adversity or struggle. However, it is those with faith that reap rewards for their faithfulness.

The rewards Wilton has reaped are all due to his obedience and being of service to others. After a brief period of unemployment, Wilton received a better paying job; God is at the center of their individual lives and their marriage, he and his wife are blessed with a successful 61 year marriage, marital strife has been kept to a minimum, and a greater attraction toward God comes over him when enduring personal storms.

Wilton stated that prayer is the most effective tool to connect to God. He encouraged, "Pray every day in no specific technique. Just talk to Him because He hears you. Give gratitude for all things, forgive yourself, forgive others, and most importantly, accept everyone for who they are."

The true character of God is always unconditional, supportive, and kind. We are all sinners and no, we do not need to be saintly in order for Heaven to be revealed. Human qualities and human values combined in, on, and around God demonstrate faith without making you become a slave to God or to a religion. This is when Heaven will be created here on earth and eternal Heaven is assured.

Words of Encouragement

"Why do you feel the way you do? What makes your heart so hard? There's a better way to look at things and there's a satisfaction that comes with it. I know what you may be thinking, 'I'm satisfied with my life.' But, are you really? Change your attitude in having faith and trust in others who accept Christ and the Bible as the handbook on life. They live improved and happier lives because of it. I stress my satisfaction in knowing that you're doing something right, but there can be a change in the way you see people and the way you understand them too. You are a good person, but you can be a better person.

"As far as getting into your future, dwell on things of the present for it could help and prevent some of the blow ups and failures that you have had every once in a while. Something will tell you in here," Wilton pointed to his heart and continued, "That you shouldn't do that certain something. I promise you will find an inner satisfaction in every area of your life that can only be found in God whether it's at home or at work. You're not going to completely change, but there are certain aspects of your life that should be different, could improve, and you know what they are. You may not want to face them, but you know this truth. You would feel so much better about yourself."

– **Wilton Ward**

8

If you ask it in my name, I shall do it
(John 14:14)

Many of us have been playing the game of "Pass the Buck" since childhood, hiding and blaming others for our shortcomings, failures, dishonesties, and struggles. While another person's words or actions can sometimes cause less than joyous circumstances in our lives, most often these conditions are self-inflicted; and, rather than admit our flaws to ourselves, much less God, we do our best to conceal our faults and blemishes hoping that no one else will notice.

Fully submitting ourselves to God in every facet of our life – minute by minute, hour by hour, and day by day – is difficult. Unfortunately, a mass majority of believers live faith with one foot in and one foot out making convenient excuses for not establishing a complete relationship with God. A half-full relationship with God is truly half-empty and results in diminished blessings and unanswered prayers.

Born and raised in Annapolis, Maryland, Kelley Clark is the eldest child of two. Regardless of periodic fussing and fighting with her brother while growing up, she credits God as her encouraging cheerleader in life.

Kelley's dad was a police officer, one of the first black officers in Annapolis back then, and her mother worked for the Navy for 27 years. Both parents put a lot of time into raising her and her brother by teaching them strong values about work ethics, treatment of people, and the limitless quality of life. They encouraged Kelley and her brother to work hard and to aspire to do whatever they wanted to do – if they made the choice to do so. They were to set their course and work hard for it.

Kelley commented that her childhood was weird and difficult compared to her brother's. She liked school, but she spent a good deal of her teen years reading books and watching television rather than making friends and playing outside.

As for her demeanor, it was frequently compared to the demeanor of her father. Just like him, her temper was short, she possessed little tact when speaking what was on her mind, and when she tired of talking out disputes with her adversaries, she swung punches at them. Her mom used to tell her, "When you see trouble brewing, leave; but, if you can't run from it, deal with it."

The truth is, a good majority of the time you can see trouble bearing down on you like a freight train; but, running away is not always an option.

One day, while in her junior high school gym class, a girl exchanged words with Kelley. Although she did everything she was taught to do to keep the exchange from snowballing, it got worse. Before she knew it, an altercation took place. It lasted maybe five minutes and when it was over, Kelley's shirt was torn and she could not stop shaking. The kids who witnessed the dispute gazed at her in shock to what they just saw: this usually quiet kid rolling around on the floor with fists flying.

A week later, another girl started to exchange words with Kelley when, to her surprise, the young woman whom she had fought the previous week stepped in and spoke up for her. Next thing anyone knew, those girls were in a brawl with one another. Kelley walked away wondering what had just happened because no one had ever done that for her.

By the time she entered college, she paid close attention to her thoughts, projected words, and how other people might react. When she started to work professionally, she was quick to observe what was going on within herself, particularly when she started to feel that she was going into self-destruct mode. Today, she is wise to the fact that there are going to be people who will and will not like her no matter what she does or fails to do. All that she can do, all that any of us can do, is take care of her mind and her heart.

As a child, church was a fundamental structure for Kelley's family – a practice that always made her heavily contemplate life whenever she listened to the sermons; however, regardless of the wonderful, inspiring, and encouraging messages, faith continued to remain on the surface of her soul. She appreciated God, but did not embrace Him into her heart or choices and habits of everyday life.

For a brief period in her thirties, Kelley had been in an abusive relationship that was psychologically toxic. Her boyfriend found her passion, drive, love, self-respect, and independent character irritating. In an attempt to make her become emotionally dependent upon only him for her needs and wants, boyfriend attempted to isolate her, even break her away from her family and friends. She lived in this hell of psychological bondage until God interrupted.

While attending a church service with her boyfriend's family, the officiating bishop gave a sermon on effective praying with "The Lord's Prayer" as the blueprint. He stated that prayers should be as individual, unique, and personal as each and every one of us are and as the bishop continued speaking, the Holy Spirit poured its presence into and over her. Immediately, she was convicted of what she had long ignored. She knew that everything she had been doing in her life up until that moment was not quite right and now, she could no longer ignore, excuse, or reason her godless choices and lifestyle. Her yearning to walk the "right" path – the path of both moral and sexual integrity – grew desperate.

Following the sermon, the bishop announced an "altar call" - a practice in which those who wish to make a new spiritual commitment to Jesus Christ do so by publicly standing up in response. All Kelley could feel, think, and hear was, "Stand up, walk forward, accept it, and don't be embarrassed. No one else is here but you and Me." Kelley stood up. Her boyfriend remained seated staring at her in wonder clueless to what her gesture meant or would foretell of their future.

Within a few short weeks, the test of genuine trust, commitment, integrity, and submission to God presented itself when Kelley's everyday comforts, habits, and surroundings came to a moral collision. The relationship between her and her boyfriend figuratively headed south like a freight train and as trouble between them heated up, she discovered that she was pregnant.

One day, several months into her pregnancy, she stood in front of a mirror and gradually studied her body's growing change. When her eyes – the windows to the soul - met their reflection, she said out loud, "He's not going to be here in May. You had better be prepared to do this by yourself."

Life with him involved too much drama and although it was clear for quite some time that he did not want to be with her, he let Kelley know this truth in a very nasty manner. With courage and strength, she told him, "I didn't grow up living with this and I'm not about to now. You can leave." Days later, home consisted of Kelley, her dog Jett, and four months later, her son, Gabriel.

Gabriel's name means "God's messenger" and she credits God for inspiring his name because her life did not change until she became pregnant. She believes that this was God's way of getting her to make the change. If she was not going to do it for herself, then she would do it for her child.

Every morning, before Gabriel gets dressed, he climbs on Kelley's lap, they give each other a big hug, and Kelley prays. She prays for them, for others, and for the things that result in evenings at home with love, respect, and a feeling of safety and security.

There are those of us who have difficulty seeing ourselves in need of God, but we need to hold ourselves accountable. She emphasized, "Accept that some things aren't right. Feel and know that you haven't been doing things right. Stop justifying your actions and just take responsibility for your less than honorable thoughts and decisions because as accountability for yourself comes forth, so does forgiveness. Forgive yourself and don't worry what other people say because the relationship you build with God is truly your private personal relationship with Him and no one else. Then, pray on it. I don't care where you do it or how you do it. Just trust and hand all your various concerns and struggles in life over to God. If it helps, hand it over through a symbolic gesture. Write your concern down on a piece of paper, place it in an ashtray, and burn it.

"A good majority of us don't realize that God does in fact answer all prayers. Most of the time, it comes in pieces through remarks and conversations from people or feelings of déjà vu. We each need to pay closer attention to how situations play out in the long run. The pieces of information you get will fit together like a puzzle – and there's your answer!

"When you hear people say that God doesn't give you what you want, He gives you what you need, I encourage everyone to find comfort in this and be more observant of situations. Only God knows how much and what kind of information that you can deal with in your present situation. When my relationship with God began, not only did my life transform, so did the relationships with everyone around me."

Kelley is now happily married to a God-filled man. She declared that if it were not for her relationship with Christ, she would not have been brave enough to step out in faith to meet someone new much less see where a relationship would go.

Aside from the initial fear of starting a new relationship, she refrained from doing something that she and a lot of women are guilty of: She did not chase this man, she did not pursue the relationship, she did not look for motives, she did not question why or why not, she did not ask about his past, and she did not judge him. Because she strived to walk the path of God's Word, she paid strict attention to what Biblical marriages look like. In the Bible, a woman never chases after a man for marriage or a healthy relationship. It is the man who both finds and asks the woman for her hand because God moves the man's heart.

As people and believers who crave relationships while living in obedience to God's Word, we are to trust where God places our feet, trust that He has each of us where He wants us, and trust that we are there for a reason. As trouble-free and strong as this all sounds, it's easier said than done. Kelley still has fleeting moments where she questions another person's motives debating whether or not they are right or wrong, but as she has matured, lived, seen, and experienced enough as a woman of faith, she now knows that not everything is personally directed at her. If a person does not like her, she accepts it. If she experiences people who lack compassion, integrity, and kindness, she strives to be the better person. No matter what someone else may do or say, she does not take it personally.

Words of Encouragement

"If not for God, you wouldn't be here! Attend church as often as you can, fellowship with other believers, and ask questions. Hear someone else's interpretation and feelings of what God's Word means because God does exist. Get past the church politics and the emphasis of what you look like when you walk through the doors. God doesn't care about your fine clothes, jewelry, or perfume. He's looking at your heart. Forgive yourself, forgive me, and forgive everyone around you. Quiet yourself and look within because that's where God is."

– **Kelley Clark**

9

> For He made Him who knew
> no sin to be sin for us,
> that we might become the righteousness
> of God in Him
> (2 Corinthians 5:21)

An old adage says, "God writes straight with crooked lines," implying that something good can come from something bad. Mulling this over brings forth the conclusion that these so-called "crooked lines" actually refer to the experiences of disappointment, sadness, fear, anger, and rejection that we all have. Along with living our everyday experiences, we sit comfortably in front of our television sets having our minds and hearts hammered with messages and headlines of natural disasters, war, murder, adultery, abuse, and misfortune. As terrible as this all sounds and we know these to be true, there is hope and yes, it involves God.

On many occasions, He presents us with opportunities to engage our mind and intellect toward Him, the one being far greater than ourselves. When we make the choice to allow these difficulties to turn our full attention toward Him, the pain weighing us down lightens. So, give thanks in all things – not just when life is sailing along smoothly. By asking God on a daily basis to grant you wisdom and courage for your living days, God will save you from your weak resignation by sowing within you His strength, His patience, His wisdom, and His love. This is the power of God rebuilding.

Clarence Brown, born and raised in Bronx, New York, is the oldest child of three. In 1959, when his parents bought a small house, his family moved to St. Augustine, New York where he attended community elementary and middle schools, and then Fiorella H. LaGuardia High School of Music. It was here that he learned to play the piano and violin to appease his parents.

Raised Roman Catholic, the day of self-governing arrived and he voiced to his mother that the services of stand up, sit down, kneel, and stand up again accompanied by the Latin language were of no relevance to him and he did not want to go to that church anymore. With reluctance but understanding, she accepted his decision. This was the beginning of what he refers to as his "wilderness" days.

After graduation and at the leadership of his father, Clarence moved from the Bronx to the deep south of Georgia during the 1960s era of intense counterculture movements of civil rights, freedom of speech, feminism, antiwar, gay liberation, sexual revolution, drugs, and film to attend Moorehouse College. Quite often Clarence would ask his father, "Why? Help me with this please. Why here?" His father always replied, "Because I said so!"

In due course, Clarence dropped out of college. The repercussions of this deposited a very big strain on their father-son relationship that lasted for quite some time. Luckily, Clarence had the good fortune of receiving an internship at the Office of Economic Opportunity, an antipoverty organization that does youth work across the region. Working for this organization entailed the constant assistance of local churches for community activities which always placed him in, at, or near a church for reasons other than the obvious. One day, a woman told him, "Son, you look like a preacher up there." With a smile and a little cynicism in his tone, Clarence replied, "I don't think so."

In 1976, Clarence married a woman whom he had known since he was nine years old. They resided in Georgia, had two boys, and made "church" a staple in their lives so that their children would have some grounding and a good moral framework.

Their pastor, a brilliant man with many PhDs, became a great friend to Clarence and because he spoke to Clarence on an intellectual level, he had tremendous influence over him. With the pastor's encouragement, Clarence went back to school and completed his college education while he continued community work for the American Cancer Society.

One rainy day, Clarence ventured out of his office to visit the volunteers. This was the same day that God did more than just give him a tap on the shoulder. He called him.

As he drove unbuckled inside his car, he was violently shoved sideways after crossing into an intersection. His car hit the curb with such force that it rebounded, overturned, and spun to a stop. Upside down, Clarence thought to himself, "You better get out of here." He climbed out the broken driver's side window frame. Outside his car, he stood up, reached into his pocket for a cigarette and lighter to calm his nerves, and realized that not only was his jacket torn, but parts of his pants were missing too. In disbelief, Clarence sat down on the curb, looked up to the heavens, and said, "God, you now have my full, complete, and undivided attention." Clarence could have easily lost a limb or his life that day; only God knows how he survived.

After being examined and released from the hospital, his wife picked him up and together they continued his quest to visit the volunteers. For the entire remainder of the day, complete strangers approached him everywhere they went and asked, "When are you getting into the church?" Clarence and his wife looked at each other in astonishment after each and every comment. Slowly, they knew the Divine implication behind every remark and by the end of the day, he told her, "Okay, I think this is it!" She agreed.

Immediately after graduating college, Clarence began seminary school and never looked back. He believes that he would be a pastor regardless of how he got there, but fervently admits that the car accident and comments that followed that particular day were the catalysts in his expeditious walk with God.

Clarence often cautions others to refrain from giving their testimony on faith with "some weird God story." However, he firmly concludes that it is in our moments of spiritual transcendence that the presence of God is confirmed giving us confidence in our faith although they may be inexplicable to others.

Desperate to make sense of this "calling" upon his life, Clarence beseeched God for answers. Deep in prayer, an upward spiral feeling came over him and when it stopped he was in the presence of a dazzling light so bright that he could not keep his eyes affixed to its radiance. Although he may have been able to turn his eyes away, he could not turn his heart. From this light emanated an intense almost euphoric emotion of love and sense of peace like never experienced in life. It was here, in this moment of searching, that the physical, intellectual, and rational truth of God firmly affixed itself to Clarence's soul.

Faith does not exclude you from the same struggles, attacks, and tragedies that afflict others. During these times, fulfilling the call to be angry and yet not "sin" can be difficult. When asked about times of adversity and perseverance, Clarence shared that our anger is usually born from what we feel that we need, want, and deserve yet have not received or achieved.

Clarence declared two core reasons why many people today, especially men, have difficulty trusting and believing in God much less their need of Him. He said, "We are born "hard-wired ignorant" and culture teaches suppression. We are taught to be self-sufficient, strong, and to lean on no one but ourselves. The results from these concepts unfortunately result in our inability to feel, engage, and surrender further inhibiting God much less our intimacy with another person.

He said, "Early on, most of us receive programming that our world can be cold and cruel; that the agenda people have is to take advantage of us. Our elders teach us that we have to stand up, stand tall, and stand strong, but the truth is this: the remarkable quality of any faith-filled journey involves surrender. It is giving up, giving in, and giving over. It is the willing choice to listen and be directed. These concepts of surrender are hard things for a man to grasp since most of his life has been programmed a certain way. This "way" must be broken and brokenness is a hard thing."

"Nobody's hurt!" is a phrase used by some. It implies, "Take me as I am, take it or leave it. This is me, faults and all." You can come to God and He will receive you just as you are. In our economy of grace, we believe that God works within us long before we ever realize that we need Him. That is the great gift of conviction which leads to the possibility of conversion.

Words of Encouragement

"I am praying for you that you might find your way in God and that you might find the path that God wants for you. Some of you will have to be stripped from every kind of self-sufficiency. You will have to spiral down to the rock bottom of life before you can hear Him. Yes, it's painful, but you need to be okay with that because this is what it takes to hear God's voice clearly. This is where the most passionate of passionate proclaimers come from (e.g., ex-convicts, drug addicts, abusers, and alcoholics). Many people including church people may be nice but they are not deeply passionate about their beliefs and walk with God until they have been delivered from something in their lives. Ask for deliverance and see the change."

– **Pastor Clarence Brown**

10

> And we know that in all things
> God works for the good of those who love Him,
> who have been called according to His purpose
> (Romans 8:28)

~~~~~~~

    The Apostle Paul emphasized the "good" as something far more precious and valuable than the luxuries of comfort and wealth that we all strive to attain. What he spoke of was the supernatural – the Holy Spirit - Who provides us the faith we are unable to muster up on our own while in the midst of various trials, struggles, and storms of life. God provided a way for us to be living children, hence the phrase "born again", where the human soul is regenerated with His Spirit inside us.

    George and his wife Evelyn share their home with her mother, Annemarie. The rapport amongst the three of them is one of great respect not just because they are family, but because of a particular life event that brought all three of them to the brink of spiritual death. Although their faith is unwavering, sure, nurtured, and adhered, it was not always like that.

    Originally born and raised in Germany, Annemarie grew up in a loving home with a firm foundation of godly faith, morals, and integrity at its core.

When she was a young woman, she fell in love with a military man whom she married and eventually had children with. Their oldest child, Thomas, was born in Germany and when he was just five months old, the three of them moved to the United States of America where her husband served in the U.S. military. Stationed in New York, Annemarie gave birth to their second child, Evelyn, two years later.

After 16 years of marriage, her husband became deathly ill and died. Young, widowed, and single at the age of 39, Annemarie's dependency and faith on God as her provider, protector, refuge, and strength grew increasingly strong and deep as each day passed and as she raised two children on her own. She kept her hope and heart attentive to His promise, "Therefore we do not lose heart. Though outwardly we are wasting away, yet inwardly we are renewed day by day. Our affliction, as seen from God's eternity, is for just a moment and is working for us a far more exceeding and eternal substance of glory while we remain in faith The things that are seen are temporary, but the things that are not seen are eternal." (2 Corinthians 4:16-18)

Before long, God graced Annemarie and her children with a good and godly man. His name was Johann and just like Annemarie, he also had two children from his marriage, Kevin and Jason.

When he and Annemarie met, Johann worked as a tool crib attendant and as soon as he divorced, he and Annemarie dated. Nine years later, after every one of their children had grown into adults and were living away from home, they married.

In 1994, Johann and his sons were propelled into a twisted entanglement of circumstances that involved depression, misery, rage, and eventually, murder.

His son, Kevin, lost his job and as days, weeks, and months passed without employment, his wife filed for a separation. Then unemployed, separated, and homeless, Kevin's spirit sank lower than low.

In a gesture of compassion and brotherly love, Jason moved Kevin into his home with his family. Sadly, no matter how loving, supportive, encouraging, and helpful the structure of family was around Kevin, depression had a ruthless hold him; and, the hell in Kevin's mind gravitated onto everyone in the house.

Uncomfortable and fearful, Jason planned a much needed vacation that did not include Kevin. In an effort to not leave him feeling abandoned, Jason phoned their father, Johann, to house-sit with Kevin while he and his family were away. Johann agreed. However, the rest of the family – Annemarie, George, and Evelyn – had their reservations. Evelyn even took it upon herself to phone her step-brother, Jason. She pleaded with him to either put his vacation off for another time or to get someone else to house-sit. Her suggestions and pleas were resisted.

As scheduled, Johann kissed Annemarie goodbye and went to Jason's. A week later, two uniformed police officers greeted George and Evelyn at their front door at 2:30 in the morning. Just as George asked the officers if there was a problem, Evelyn emerged and frantically asked, "He killed him, didn't he?!"

The officer's reply informed them that when Jason and his family returned home from vacation, there was obvious evidence that an altercation of some kind had taken place throughout the house, neither Kevin nor Johann could be found, and Johann's car was also missing. Jason phoned the police immediately and regrettably, investigators discovered Johann's body buried under leaves behind Jason's house the next day. Based on information given by family, Kevin became the suspect and an "All-Points

Bulletin" was issued for his apprehension. A manhunt was under way.

Later that morning, George and Evelyn picked up Annemarie and the three of them drove to Jason's. As they pulled up to his neighborhood, many police cars were along the street and in several neighbors' driveways.

The following day, two police officers in Poughkeepsie, New York, spotted Kevin. They arrested him and took him to their local police station for questioning. Kevin's demeanor was lucid and carefree except for when he was in the interrogation room. He complained that that the room itself made him uncomfortable. To keep him talking, the officers moved Kevin into a larger room with air-conditioning, a leather recliner, a sofa, a loveseat, a television, and a fan. Then, they ordered him a pizza.

Informed of his Miranda Rights, which he voluntarily waived, Kevin confessed to killing his father. Immediately, the New Hampshire authorities were notified and in no time flat, they arrived in Poughkeepsie with a warrant for Kevin's arrest and extradition.

Upon entering the holding room, they found him lying comfortably on the sofa watching television. The detectives introduced themselves, explained why they were there, and with Kevin's permission and agreement, they tape recorded their interview about his father death. Again, Kevin was informed of his Miranda Rights, again, he waived them, and again, he confessed to Johann's murder. At the trial, he was convicted of second-degree murder and sentenced to 27 years to life in prison.

Although Annemarie's pain of such personal loss was immense, the event remarkably never shook or moved her faith in God. If anything, she was initially mad at Johann for leaving her. All she wanted was to be with him wherever he was.

Two weeks later, the breakdown she had long ignored emerged. She cried 'her heart out' and then, wondered if she was somehow responsible for Johann's demise. She went to God in prayer. On her knees, she confessed and sought His forgiveness for everything she may and may not have been aware of throughout her entire life that could have ever disappointed Him. Then, just as any good parent does for any innocent child in so much pain, God embraced her. An immeasurable sense of warmth, love, and peace came over her. By God's grace, she recognized it as the Holy Spirit encompassing her as He had done so many times before. The weight of heartbreak did not cease, but it lightened.

Some things in life can be patched up, repaired, rebuilt, and redone while there are some things too severe, too painful, and too shattered to be pulled back together. While it can be easy to emotionally crumble, God created a joyous art form called *encouragement* to help us out of out pit of hopelessness. So, rather than keep an attitude of "can't be fixed", remember that with God - all lives, all wounds, and all circumstances can be made new.

Once the murder was publicized, George found himself the recipient of additional loss that left him in a state of greater confusion and collapse. His once thriving and successful computer business went bust leaving him penniless and unable to pay bills. The only clients who showed any kind of professional loyalty and/or personal compassion to what he, Evelyn, and Annemarie were going through were the ones considered friends. Then, as if life weren't handing them enough exertion, they had to endure the emotional turmoil of Kevin's trial.

One afternoon, George sat in his shop overwhelmed with the emotions of anger, agitation, worry, and despair. He was so furious that he believed the death penalty was the equal and justified penalty for what Kevin had done. Feeling as though the world from underneath his feet had been yanked out, George supplicated God in a loud desperate voice, "Dear Lord, please help me!"

Without delay, a sense of calm and peace came over him. Two days later, "good" things started to emerge. One particular client of George's purchased all of his test equipment and benches which gave George some cash in his pocket and then, the client offered him a full-time job which George graciously took.

The following day and thereafter, George's business competitors phoned and purchased all of his remaining equipment from chairs and spare parts to his client list. George and his family were lifted up and out of their financial slam; and ironically, George's new job placed him within a one hour drive from where the trial was being held. With Evelyn at his side, George made sure she was at the trial every single day in case anything was stated incorrectly. He credits God and that single act of genuine prayer where he placed his troubles at the feet of Jesus for all the blessings that followed. God's timing was quick too.

During the trial, Jason attempted to blame his father for his own slaying. Perhaps it was a desperate attempt to restore a sense of respect and honor to his own family, but Jason's claims caused a greater division amongst everyone in the family.

With a heavy heart, George said, "It should not have happened. None of it! Johann loved Kevin. He loved both of his sons and this tragedy affected all of us. You see, Johann was not just my father-in-law, he was my best friend. When I started my company, I was working seven days a week to get it off the ground as any new business owner does. Times were tight and when we needed something, Evelyn had to watch every penny.

"Whenever Johann and Annemarie came to visit, Johann would cut the lawn, make repairs, and do anything else we needed while Annemarie cooked us meals. They were always with us supporting us with whatever we did. All of us got along with one another really well. We ate, talked, laughed, went out, and even made beer together. His son took someone very precious from me and I still get angry about it."

Evelyn interjected and as she spoke, tears filled her eyes. She said, "I'll never forget that day as long as I live. The eerie part is that just two days before the police showed up at our door, I had a dream with Johann in it. My stepfather walked up to me and with a big smile said, 'Ev, look, I'm not in pain anymore. It's over and I'm not in pain.' The next morning I shared this dream with George because it felt so real."

Evelyn paused, wiped away her tears, and with composure she continued, "Yes, what happened was awful. If I could turn the clocks back and change the situation, Johann would still be here with all of us. Nevertheless, after all we've been through and the changes that have taken place, both the loss and the result are, in a sense, bitter-sweet. Many valuable lessons have been learned and a greater amount of love has triumphed in our family. I have learned to pay closer attention to my feelings. All the uneasiness that I had felt prior to Johann's leaving and then the dream days later, they were signs of what was to come. I have also learned that when our kids become adults, our job at parenting is done. Our heart will always be there, but we are to back off, stay out of their business, and let them be responsible for their choices no matter how good or bad those choices are. We can offer advice but ultimately, it's our kid's decision whether or not to take it. We all make our own mistakes and pay the consequences, whatever they are.

"The greatest lesson of all has been to draw closer to God in times of suffering. It's not God's fault that bad and evil things happen to us. It's ours because we are a fallen species born into a fallen world. To be blurred from divinity, fall victim to pain, and give up on life are the successful works of Satan. God is merciful and God is love. He gets us through, He helps us rebuild, and He rescues us when we endure the loss of a loved one at the hands of another."

Her words made George remember that when the police located Johann's car, a map with fuel receipts of Kevin's escape route were scattered all over the passenger seat. The handwritten words, "The devil made me do it!" were found inside the map.

George, Evelyn, and Annemarie all stated that as a world, we should strive to acquire the same characteristics of Jesus in loving one another, including our enemies.

Although George still has moments of struggle with forgiveness today, the intensity of his rage and hurt are not what they once were. As for Evelyn and Annemarie, their minds, hearts, and souls are free from hatred, anger, or judgment toward Kevin. They know that the true "Day of Judgment" will come for him as it will for every one of us. We will all stand before God to answer for our choices and actions.

George and Evelyn recently celebrated their 30th wedding anniversary and as they held hands during this interview process, they reflected on their previous years as a couple and together, they gave relationship advice.

In the interim of their marriage, neither one of them has ever disrespected the other, but before their union, George admitted, he had a very chauvinistic and vain thought process about himself and women. He believed that he could have any woman he wanted so, he used to look up and down at every woman that passed by him and decide on their attractiveness or lack thereof. Oddly, when George met Evelyn, he took her in with his eyes and thought to himself, "Nope. Not my type." Evelyn, on the other hand, never batted a single eyelid in George's direction.

One day, George's secretary asked him to make sure Evelyn was included in their "lunch group" especially if they went out to eat or dancing on the weekends because she enjoyed those activities and did not know anyone. After several lunch gatherings, George started finding Evelyn completely and utterly enjoyable. They danced, talked, laughed, and before long, George though about her a lot, especially the days she missed work or was unable to attend lunch. In time, her absence hit George like a ton of bricks. He admitted, "When she wasn't around, I missed her and I never thought about any of the other women like that!"

This revelation prompted George to share his feelings with Evelyn and when he did, he discovered that she felt the same way he did.

In the early stages of dating, George emotionally drifted away from Evelyn a couple of times due to two reasons: The disrespect of his wandering eye and his fear of commitment.

After their second break up, George said that Evelyn did the unthinkable! She dated someone else. That was when he stopped ignoring his heart and finally voiced to her that he did not want a day in his life to go by without her in it. He asked her to get married.

God is and has been the key ingredient to their successful marriage. George's covenant, focus, and loyalty to Jesus Christ as His child, a man, and husband all result in a greater sense of unity between him and Evelyn. He never possessed such a wonderful gift before.

As wonderful as their marriage is, it is not perfect. When there is a conflict between them, they both take an emotional step back from the issue, they both stop taking the problem personally, and they both soon recognize the real issue at hand. And quite often, they realize that the problem is not with each other.

The core component that makes any relationship work in a good, healthy, and happy manner is respect.

Together, they said, "Respect one another, learn each other's likes and dislikes, and by all means, never ever transmit the attitude, 'You need to become what I want,' because if you do, you're just asking for trouble."

Over the years, George has learned to not get on Evelyn's bad side and he is assured within himself that he would not be as successful as he is today without her. He expressed, "A husband should never look at his wife with resentment or disvalue. So what if your woman doesn't come to the table with money like you do! She's still a person of worth and you had better acknowledge it; otherwise, the chance of your marriage becoming a divorce statistic is likely."

Evelyn supports George the way God commands a wife to do. With encouragement, she stated, "Marriage is a partnership, not a 'one-upmanship' and for a couple to have the advantage of a successful marriage, God needs to be in the equation. With God, no one takes their life, marriage, or partner for granted."

Not only is the divorce rate in society today high, but the divorce rate amongst Christians is growing. Without pointing blame, Evelyn stated the obvious.

She said, "Most Christian marriages break up because either one or both parties turn their eyes and heart away from God. This "turning away" is injurious because it's where the breakdown occurs and where one or both souls drown in worldly lust, greed, materialism, and judgment. Ruin is inevitable."

She too enjoys the finer things in life, but by remaining focused on appreciation for what she has instead of on what she wants God showers her with all kinds of good things.

The greatest gift she maintains is His Spirit. When He moves, expands, and grows within her life, fresh faith empowers and enables her to stand firm and move mountains of adversity. God is the one who nurtures her soul and builds her faith just as He does George's and Annemarie's.

Annemarie encourages God, trust, respect, and communication between couples at all times to have a successful marriage. The Christ qualities in her first marriage of 16 years were forgiveness, resolution, and loyalty. They were all part of its structure even when the enemy of alcoholism made its way into her husband's existence. He spent years battling this demon while she battled his inebriation and violent outbursts. When the disease started to deteriorate his life, Annemarie visited with him in the hospital every day often taking the children with her in the evenings. To ease her mind when stressed, she visited the hospital chapel for prayer and responsiveness. Occasionally, she would cry out, "Lord, I don't know what to do anymore so, I give it to You." Other times, she simply sought God's solace.

In all occasions of prayer, the Lord dispensed His compassion, reassurance, peace, and love over her. When she was afraid, God gave her His peace and when her husband was in pain, God gave him His comfort.

In her second marriage of 14 years, she and Johann were equally yoked. They shared the same faith, morals, and plans for a future. Although they were both brought up to accept Christ, they each worshipped Him differently. They did what they had been conditioned to do by their religion, family, and culture.

Every Sunday morning they went their separate ways for church service. For the sake of their marriage and God, they chose to share one holiday in the year together, Christmas. On Christmas Eve, they attended services together at Annemarie's church and on Christmas Day, they attended services together at Johann's church.

George, Evelyn, and Annemarie all concur that while some people refuse to give God the acknowledgment He deserves, it is the person who has never been humbled in life that has the most difficulty embracing or respecting God much less any organized religion or belief. George said, "If you look deeply at the lives of people whose hearts are vacant of God, their lives are actually empty. That is why they jump from relationship to relationship and purchase thing after thing. They seek happiness, but this happiness is always short-lived."

When you find yourself experiencing disappointments, unmet expectations, or unreachable dreams in yourself or in someone else, strive to remember that our lives will happen the way they are supposed to. Place hope in its rightful place, with God, and you will soon discover what He has planned for you is usually far better than you could have ever planned for yourself.

Words of Encouragement

"Love the Lord with all your heart, soul, and mind because a relationship with Christ keeps you comfortable and assured of where you are going at all times. Make God the stronger priority in your life and in your relationships both in and out of the house. As a couple, pray together! Study the Bible and pray for one another's need, desire, and walk with God. Not only does prayer have the power to move mountains, but the family who prays together, stays together."
–**George Tarnovsky, Evelyn Tarnovsky,** and **Annemarie Gotsch**

11

For we are God's handiwork, created in Christ Jesus to do good works, which God prepared in advance for us to do

(Ephesians 2:10)

When I say, "I am a Christian"
I'm not shouting, "I've been saved!"
I'm whispering, "I get lost!
That's why I chose this "way"

When I say, "I am a Christian"
I don't speak with human pride
I'm confessing that I stumble—
Needing God to be my guide

When I say, "I am a Christian"
I'm not trying to be strong
I'm professing that I'm weak
And pray for strength to carry on

When I say, "I am a Christian"
I'm not bragging of success
I'm admitting that I've failed
And cannot ever pay the debt

When I say, "I am a Christian"
I don't think I know it all
I submit to my confusion
Asking humbly to be taught

When I say, "I am a Christian"
I'm not claiming to be perfect
My flaws are all too visible
But God believes I'm worth it

When I say, "I am a Christian"
I still feel the sting of pain
I have my share of heartache,
Which is why I seek His name

When I say, "I am a Christian"
I do not wish to judge
I have no authority...
I only know I'm loved" –
    "WHEN I SAY, I AM A CHRISTIAN"

By Carol Wimmer

The eldest child of seven with 16 years between her and her youngest sibling, Hannah Gibson joked that she changed diapers long before she ever had her own place, much less her own children.

Raised a devout Catholic, she credits her parents for instilling the seeds of faith, integrity, self-respect, and compassion for herself and others.

Her father's work moved the family to several different states until he chose to settle in Michigan. If you are an outdoor enthusiast, Michigan is a dream come true. You will find beaches, sand dunes, mountains, and parks where you can go sunbathing, swimming, boating, fishing, bicycling, camping, golfing, hiking, hunting, paddle sports, cross-country skiing, downhill skiing, dog sledding, snowboarding, snowmobiling, and off-road driving for off-road vehicles.

In the course of her adolescence, Hannah believed in God, but did not make Him a priority in her life. Actually, she politely confessed that she once viewed religion as nothing more than a sweet gesture and role that her parents performed.

Hannah's priorities were to be intellectually sophisticated through philosophy, art, and literature. Knowing what she knows now, her existence and health is tribute to God and her mother's devoted undertaking of daily praying.

Originally born with facial deformities, school – from elementary to college – was an emotional hell for Hannah. Many kids pointed and laughed at her. For a long time, she assumed that they hated her because of her looks and in turn, she hated herself.

One afternoon, after Hannah arrived home from school, she broke down in tears. As she lay on the sofa sobbing, her mother sat next to her, placed her hand gently upon her, and asked, "What's the matter?"

Hannah tearfully replied, "I can't take it anymore! I'm tired of being humiliated, and I can't stand the way I look!"

Surprised, yet sympathetic to her suffering, her mother affectionately told her, "It never occurred to me that you were anything but beautiful because I love you so much."

The next day, Hannah's mother took her to see a plastic surgeon and over the next several years, surgeries changed her appearance as well as her self-confidence and ability to have a social life.

While at college, Hannah met her future husband, Jeff, a fellow student. His friendship brought God to the forefront of her life as he was the only one in their circle of friends who regularly attended church. They spent hours together conversing over academics, family, life, and religion. The more time they spent together, the closer they became.

With a modest laugh, Hannah admitted that both she and Jeff each had a strong sense of pride in their intellect and knowledge about what was and was not in the Bible. Sometimes, their conversations on a particular topic of scripture got heated and turned into a debate.

The days that Jeff attended church, he always reached out and invited her to go with him. For a long time, she politely declined, but one evening, while at a friend's dorm, she spotted Jeff making his way to church. She hollered, "Hey! Off to church, are you?"

With a smile, he hollered back, "You can come with me."

Taking one last inhale off her cigarette, Hannah threw it to the ground, crushed it out, and then said, "Oh, what the hell ... I'll go."

The church he took her to was a very basic one. A little old fashioned compared to most of today's services, but the people in attendance were kind, welcoming, accommodating, and sincerely interested in everything about her. Before leaving, some of the women invited her to attend church with them to which she accepted and before she knew it, Hannah was studying the Bible with these ladies or with Jeff almost on a nightly basis.

In time, Hannah rededicated her life to God and she took her relationship with Him, Jeff, and others more serious than ever before. Eventually, her friendship with Jeff blossomed into something much more intimate and in 1988, they married. They are still married to this day and have two grown children.

Deeply reflecting on her relationship with God, Hannah asserted that, like marriage, a relationship with Christ does not just happen or stay in place on its own. In order for this relationship or any kind of relationship to be successful against disharmony or break up, we – the other half of this correlation – must be incredibly "deliberate" in nurturing its bond, growth, and essence. If we do not do this, circumstances, people, and life will easily and viciously drive a wedge down the center of a couple's relationship.

Hannah asserted that the grace of God has been demonstrated in her life, her husband's life, and their marriage every day. For better understanding of this claim, Hannah shared a very delicate time in her life when the discomforts of change and uncertainty were at hand as was God. She said, "Life was great except for my husband's job. He was under an enormous amount of pressure and I worried that the stress was going to cause him to have a heart attack. Together, we went to God in prayer and requested that He help him get a new job. Days later, my husband was presented with a government job too good to be turned down; however, there was one small catch. Taking the job meant that we had to move.

"Our initial reaction was excitement, joy, and gratitude for such a fast response to our prayers, but after we contemplated the bigger picture, our thoughts were flooded with fear, worry, and anxiety because this 'move' required us to give up our surroundings of family, church, school, friends, and the town in which we had grown up.

"To make matters worse, we were clueless as to where we were going. Metaphorically speaking, we had willingly taken our seats upon a ship headed to 'who knows where.' No one can sit back and relax in situations like that! All we wanted was to know where we were going. With this information, we could have at least researched and prepared for the weather, much less the culture if it were in fact different. I mean, would we live in the city, the suburbs, or the countryside? Anyway, my husband and I prayed on the matter both individually and together for weeks, but it wasn't until I took a day long retreat to a monastery that I remembered a very important quality of faith that I had forgotten: *'The will of God will never take you where the grace of God will not protect you.'*

"Walking the monastery grounds, I stepped in a labyrinth of sorts. Unmindful to where I was walking or turning, I got a little lost until I chose to back track my steps. That's when I was able to discover signs confirming that I was on the right path. The most interesting thing about that day was this: approximately halfway through my walk, I started feeling apprehensive about going in the right direction when out from nowhere, a dog showed up and walked alongside me until I got out of it."

There is no doubt in Hannah's heart or mind that the dog was God's sweet and kind gesture of reassuring her to not worry about her walk or their upcoming move because everything will fall into place just as it is supposed to. This experience encouraged Hannah's ministry to the world that God is accessible to everyone. "We just have to walk and trust Him." There may be some twists and turns on our paths but, when we get to where we are supposed to be, God reveals everything and it's always better than what we could have ever anticipated.

In the fall of 2010, God's will and grace took Hannah, Jeff, and their children to the forefront of adversity in the unknown once again.

Her husband's job required him to be shipped off to a location in the Middle East for six months. This obligation was bad timing because at that time, their son, Josh, had been preparing to head off to college. It meant that Hannah would be on her own supporting their son's physical, emotional, and spiritual needs as he made the transition from home to school. As she focused on him, her own support system got shallower.

At first, she considered talking to her friend Kathy, but as quickly as the idea developed, it also refrained. Hannah stated, "What was I going to do? Offload about giving up my husband for six months to a woman who lost her husband permanently to cancer?"

Everyone else she knew was in the military and she feared that their response would be, "Oh, six months. Big deal! Wait until he has to go away for two years."

Hannah felt she had no one to sympathize with her ... no one, but God that is. Recognizing Him as the main equation in their marriage encouraged her to spend a lot of time with Him in prayer. In those moments she found the comfort she had been seeking. She also recognized two important blessings in her predicament: One, she attained a greater sense of gratefulness for her husband; and two, she discovered profound quality time, one on one, with each of their kids. These blessings gave Hannah a new perspective as to what it is like and what it means to have a soul mate for life. Jeff's absence encouraged greater empathy in Hannah's heart for those who are widowed.

To nourish and nurture her faith, Hannah reads the Bible, contemplates the meaning of each Scripture, meditates, and communes with God through prayer. Just recently, she started a spiritual practice called "Praying the Hours" – a monastic practice that monks do. It has helped her establish some order in her spiritual life and she feels more of God. With affection, she said, "View prayer as seeking answers, not just favors. Talk to Him just like you talk to your best friend."

Just like the prophet Habakkuk prayed and prophesied in a time when the people of God were caught up in a crisis of religious and moral bewilderment, you too are encouraged to pray with patience, perseverance, readiness, and confidence. She said, "Do not treat God or the Scriptures with contempt. Test everything and hold onto the good, (1 Thessalonians 5:19). Then, make up your mind."

Words of Encouragement

"I've said it a million times and I'll say it a million more because it's the truth: Jesus loves you! Ask Him to show you and trust that He will be there even if you don't get an immediate sense that He is working or that He's hearing you. Hang in there and don't give up.

"As Jesus said, 'Keep on seeking; keep on asking; keep on knocking.' I'm discovering that while God wants to answer our prayers, He values a relationship far more. He's not an 'Order Fulfillment Center', He wants to come alongside us and be in relationship with us. These attributes of His love for us often matter more than the answer to prayer that we think we want – or else all these things lead up to an answer that is richer and greater that anything we could have asked for or imagined."

– **Hannah Gibson**

12

Harm none and do what you will

～～～

Only by the power of God can our heart, mind, will, and belief change into the increasing likeness of Christ. Only through a trusting relationship with God are we enabled to gather strength and the capacity to hold a positive outlook when challenges and transformation bombard our lives. So, rather than sit back and remain the victim to predicaments that are out of your control, gain the upper-hand by remembering that although you are God's creation, earth is not His realm. It's Satan's.

Sarah declared that faith is something she has been searching for. While this declaration would deter other writers for a book such as this, I found her apprehension and honesty humbling because she stands where many of us stand or have stood before. I affirm, without a doubt, that Sarah's faith is in fact established. It is the so-called "religious" label or title that she is searching for – as if the choice for a personal relationship with God needs one.

Raised in the mountains of West Virginia from the age of three, Sarah is a middle child of six. Growing up, she and her family were all very close and loyal to one other like they are today, regardless of typical sibling bickering.

As adults today, they are not in contact with each other as much as they would like to be, but the love and allegiance to one another remains and is obvious whenever they come together for family gatherings.

Sarah's home was happy and safe. Food was always on the table even if it meant that her dad had to go out and hunt for it. Living in the mountains encouraged Sarah's joy for the outdoors. She climbed trees, swam in algae-filled ponds, and rode horses with nothing more than a halter and reins made from bailing twine. When she was not on the run, she enjoyed writing short stories and drawing. This creative artistry is still with her today and you can find her artwork available for purchase at http://www.sarahhonaker.com

Both of Sarah's parents instilled the teachings of the Bible which gave their family a strong foundation of faith and belief in the divine. Primarily Christian, the family respected all religious beliefs and acknowledged all holidays. Thanksgiving and Christmas were wonderful celebrations as was Passover though no one in the family was Jewish. As a family tradition, her mother always made the symbolic gesture of faith and thankfulness by adding an extra place setting at the table for Jesus.

As for religious encouragement, Sarah stated, "Mom and Dad gave us the gift of solid faith and as a child, nothing gave me a greater sense of security other than my parents and knowing that God was always watching over me, protecting me, and loving me unconditionally no matter what I did or thought. As a bonus, He holds a spot for me – for everyone actually – in Heaven when I die."

Whenever she experienced night terrors as a child, she discovered that when she prayed to God, called on her Guardian Angel, and envisioned God's white light of protection surrounding her, the fears that bombarded her mind lost their power and hold. Once, she actually saw an Angel standing over her with a sword in its hand, like a watchtower.

As a small child, Sarah was given a vision of Heaven. She stated, "It was one of the most vivid and realistic dreams of my childhood and to this day, I cherish its memory.

"I was on a pathway adorned with the sparkles of rubies, emeralds, turquoise, and pearls underfoot. Ahead of me, I could hear the cheerful gurgling of water from the crystal clear stream which flowed between the tall sweet-smelling trees. There were dogs, puppies, and many other animals playing together and running around me as I walked along the path. Alongside me was a Presence that emanated safety, love, and guidance. In the background was a steady uninterrupted orchestra similar to the sound of birds but not exactly, bells but a little different, and wind but more. When I woke up, all I could think about were Angels singing."

Sarah shared this vision with her mom and instead of pointing out its impracticalities or absurdities, her mom instructed her to write it down. As Sarah wrote, she asked her mom if animals really went to Heaven. Her mother told her that God saw it fit to show her Heaven with animals in it. So yes, there must be animals in Heaven.

Sarah's mom has that paper to this day and periodically she pulls it out and discusses its content with Sarah as a reminder of faith.

Sarah and her family faithfully attended church every Sunday. That is, until there was a nasty debate over the interpretation of Scripture between her father and their pastor. The dispute resulted in the pastor making a convicting remark that no one in their family made very good stewards of God because they questioned everything. Sarah walked away from this incident with the life lessons that, "Most people in authority don't like having their knowledge on a subject questioned or challenged, and if a person can't ask questions about the Bible, then perhaps they shouldn't accept 'It' just because the man behind the pulpit said 'It'."

From then on, the family held devotional services at home amongst themselves and their neighbors. They read the Bible every night and followed up with discussions of how each verse reflected life as they knew it for themselves and for others. With joy, Sarah said, "Bible study at home was fun! My dad made a game out it, sort of like Trivial Pursuit. He would enthusiastically ask, 'What were the names of three men burned alive in the furnace?' My sisters, brothers, and I would shout out, 'Shadrach, Abednigo, and Meshach!' When we remembered and announced the fourth figure – "God" who was also in those flames – my dad's face radiated immense satisfaction and joy into the entire room."

Sarah grew up differently than most kids of her generation. She was homeschooled and for many years the family did not have a television. Reading was greatly encouraged as were outdoor activities along with writing, drawing, and the use of their imaginations.

Homeschooled, Sarah got straight A's when taking the scholastic tests. She credited her mother's teaching and the absence of distractions in her surroundings for her ability to ace those tests. In other words, unlike kids in public schools, she and her siblings never experienced bullying from their peers. Excellence was constantly encouraged and considered normal.

When television finally invaded their home, it was in the form of a 13" black-and-white television set with channel, volume, and power knobs. Although it took a while to get used to it, television led to one of Sarah's favorite family activities: commentating.

Her dad would put on a television show, turn the volume all the way down, and then provide his own dialogue to the programming. Then, she and the rest of the family would take turns providing voice-overs with some hilarious results. When it was over, her dad would wrap up their time with his infamous rendition of the Looney Tunes character Elmer Fudd, "I'm gonna get you, you wascally wabbit!" This always sent her and her siblings into profuse giggles.

By the time Sarah was ready for sixth grade, her entire family's everyday conduct with school, home, and income had changed. Her father's small business closed, the family moved, and Sarah started to attend public school. To help with their finances, she took an after-school job when she was just 15 years old. She washed dishes at an upscale German restaurant from 4 p.m. until closing which usually lasted long after midnight.

In due course, her parents' relationship started to suffer as did Sarah's school grades, self-esteem, spirit, faith, and personal attempts at making good decisions. With regret Sarah said, "This was a time when we all should have fallen back on our strong foundation of faith, but we didn't."

Within time, Sarah turned away from organized religion altogether. She gave herself over to a life of worldliness, materialism, and desire with a long line of both male and female partners. She became the very definition of the word "promiscuous." While she may have temporarily enjoyed herself at times, the afflictions of self-loathing, unhappiness, and zero self-worth constantly plagued her. At the tender age of 17, she married.

Paradoxically, her in-laws were devout Christians as she once was. While faith was at the center of their lives, it was all a superficial act for Sarah and her husband. In fact, his parents' hearts would have exploded if they had known every aspect of his behavior. Her husband drank, cursed, fornicated, and digested drugs. He also carried within him the attitude, "What they don't know won't hurt them". He made sure his parents only saw what he wanted them to see.

Regardless of how quiet Sarah kept her demeanor, a crossroad between spiritual truth and sin presented itself. No longer was she able to lead a deceitful or duplicitous life and she voiced this to her husband. His reply was one of exoneration and persuasion. He claimed that one behavior need not exclude the other and that his discretionary activities were not interfering with his beliefs, religious obligations, church attendance, and family affairs. Easily persuaded, Sarah followed his lead; however, two years later, they divorced.

Single, she continued her self-indulgent behavior until her life was sorrowfully interrupted the morning of September 3, 2002. She received a phone call that her dad had been struck and killed on his motorcycle the evening before.

As she recalled this tragedy, the flames of grief and guilt reignited the pain of his loss. For a long time, Sarah's heart was heavily burdened with regret because on that particular night, at that particular hour, she had been out with some random guy whom she had just met at a bar. When her family needed her, she had intentionally made herself unavailable due to her own decadence.

The "man" who had accidentally killed her father was never charged with anything more than a ticket for failing to yield. Not once – *ever* – did the "man" express any kind of explanation, remorse, or compassion to her family for their loss. His lack of empathy, concern, or consideration harbored intense hatred for him and his entire ethnic group inside her.

During her time in bereavement, Sarah met a gentleman who was and is her saving grace. They moved to a tiny private island in the Caribbean – white silk sands, tropical breezes, vibrant perfumed foliage, and soothing nights of nothing more than the rhythmic surf and God. Healing and solitude began and in 2011, they married.

The frustration of "two steps forward and one step back" affected Sarah's efforts when it came to developing her emotional solidity.

Sarah's personal experiences have led her to the conclusion that "when we stop fighting the entire holistic idea and truly allow God into our lives, mountains of difficulties that we have not been able to overcome by our own efforts are either moved out of the way entirely or God gets us over them." She encouraged the importance of ridding our inner demons – ego, pride, and control – to ensure our freedom of offense no matter what happens or fails to happen around or to us. She warned, "If we don't rid ourselves of these personal power trips, we will continue to suffer, mostly with disappointments due to our own false expectations."

Just like you, Sarah has experienced faith at its fullest and at its barrenness. She admitted that her days of spiritual dryness were actually due to her own abandonment and transgressions against God. When we have personal days of dryness, we need to honestly ask and answer two very important questions to ourselves: Is it you who turned your face from God? Or, are you into the relationship with Him for what you can get out of it instead of loving Him for His own sake?

As you contemplate your answers, remember a few truths:

- It is Satan who puts God on trial in our lives which affects our thoughts, words, choices, and actions all of which trickle into our relationship with Him and others.

- Human wisdom, no matter how good it sounds, cannot fathom the ways of God.

- Only God can satisfy your craving for counsel, comfort, and deliverance because wisdom is found in God alone.

- Undeserved suffering has no easy answer.

- God is not obligated to explain everything to us.

Sarah smiled and said, "When life is handing out lemons, this is the time for you to become quiet, reserved, and lean in on God closer than ever for His Spirit, power, strength, love, and perseverance."

Sarah's relationship with God is as unique and individual as she is. With her faith is deep, her heart is loyal, her intentions are sincere, and she insists that prayer is the most effective and intimate method to connect with God. Her prayers sometimes consist of silence and other times, voice.

In silence, God's presence is felt and she finds content, in soft exchanges, the petitions of love and thankfulness are expressed, and in speaking, she usually expresses her personal views and advice on how a particular aspect of life or humanity could possibly have been programmed differently.

As people, we are supposed to live in harmony with one another. We should do "good" things without expecting recognition or reward. When we refrain from bragging, our actions – no matter how small or grand – affect the world and lives around us in a positive way beyond our comprehension and when a person is allowed to share their experiences, thoughts, and feelings unconditionally, they usually realize that the answer they have been searching for has been in front of them the entire time.

As for labeling her with a practicing denomination, she refuses to "act" out the motions of any organized religion until she finds a denomination that parallels her experiences with God. She believes that learning about many spiritual paths is part of a person finding God. No matter what a person practices, the center must be God and nothing else. She said, "As Christians, it's fine and good to offer information on what you believe and gently steer someone toward faith in Jesus Christ, but you should absolutely not, under any condition, condemn another person simply because they worship God in another manner. We are human, we are all His creation which is good, and God installed free will within us."

Words of Encouragement

"God (the divine) is a real force and can be a source of great comfort through life's trials. Do not fence yourself off from His love and light by allowing the ideas and rigid definitions of others dictate what form your faith should take. Do not obsess over the 'right' labeling.

"Your relationship with God is personal to you and *only you*. As the 19th-century Indian teacher Ramakrishna said, 'One should not think, "My religion alone is the right path and other religions are false." God can be realized by all paths because it is enough to have a sincere yearning for Him. Infinite are the paths and infinite are the opinions.'" The divine is all and all are the divine ... *you* are the divine."

— **Sarah (Honaker) Hampton**

13

Those who wait on the Lord
shall renew their strength.
They shall mount up with wings like eagles.
They shall run and not be weary.
They shall walk and not faint
(Isaiah 40:31)

~~~

The dimensions of God's judgment involve the promise of forgiveness, comfort, and restoration. In the book of Isaiah, you are reminded that the entirely surrendered soul is the soul that hopes and trusts in the Lord at all times as He is the one who strengthens, helps, and upholds you with His righteous hand. Securing yourself to this truth literally provides your soul with the "wings" that so many of you have cried out for from time to time. These wings free you from the bondage of disruption, irritation, and unhappiness which strive to overpower you. These wings also enable His Spirit to silence your mental chatter so that you may see and hear the guidance and blessings He desires to pour over you. Then, and only then, can you draw in "Living Water" from the spiritual well of God to nourish your spiritual birth and growth.

Jimmy Pate, the eldest child of three, grew up on

a family ranch in the Texas Hill Country. The small town of 300 in which he lived did not provide many places for entertainment, so life for him and many of the town's people consisted of church, sports, and special events. These activities kept living unpretentious and simple. "Life was good."

Along with his family's personal exemplifications and words of encouragement, Jimmy stated that he couldn't recall a time in his childhood when an interest, hobby, or pursuit did not focus on or around the foundation of his faith. In addition to church services, Sunday school, Bible school, and his participation in the 'Royal Ambassadors', a church youth group, the ranch he grew up on occasionally served as a gathering place for community, school, and religious events.

The vast picturesque foothills of the ranch enabled Jimmy to roam their land safely and stimulated his love for the outdoors. On his adventures, he frequently discovered seashells and marine-creature fossils inside rusty-colored rocks. Without an ocean or body of water nearby, these discoveries supported everything that he had ever heard, read, or learned about the Bible as truth. He said, "The ranch was a great place to grow up, especially for a boy."

Always surrounded by family, friends, and role models who all encouraged and nurtured faith, it wasn't until he attended a church revival at the age of nine that the personal allure of Jesus Christ truly caught his attraction. Jimmy willingly invited God to come into his life. The experience was deep, lovely, and life-changing.

Loyal, faithful, and reliable are both his professional and personal traits and reputation. For the past 27 years, he has worked as a coach and a teacher, professions that have collectively allowed him and his family the pleasure of traveling and living in several locations all over Texas.

Not too long ago, during one of his tenures in a small town, he and his family became very close friends with their church pastor and its attendees. It was there that they learned how to really love – and be loved. A family within the church whom he affectionately referred to as his "singing parents" observed and acknowledge Jimmy's gift of voice - the tone and melody of an Angel. They encouraged him to sing beyond just sitting in the pews. This was when Jimmy heard God's call for "all" of him and Jimmy gladly responded. He said, "This is the place where God got me off the sidelines and drew me close to Him so that I could truly begin to walk with Him. Since then, so many other things have happened – unexplainable things - which only God could have orchestrated by His grace. There's no doubt that I was in the right place at the right time doing the right thing."

Today, Jimmy remains a social studies teacher but dropped his profession as a coach to pursue music ministry for the Lord. He is now the music leader at his church in Aledo, Texas.

In December 2012, Jimmy and his wife, Sherry, celebrated their 28th wedding anniversary with their two grown daughters. He stated that the qualities of honor, admiration, and praise found in his relationship with God are also found in their marriage. Both he and Sherry view their relationship and marriage as a privilege, a gift that respects and honors God as well as each other.

Just as God created him to be and the Bible says who he is, Jimmy is the man, leader, provider, and protector of his family although, there are times when he gladly hands over some of the decision making to her as she has more influence and knowledge on various circumstances than he.

Their marriage is about working together and working it out no matter what without governing, controlling, or dictating the other because God never promised us a life without troubles. He did promise that we would not experience more than we could handle.

Every relationship goes through rough times and situations, and it is those who believe in God and keep Him at the center of their marriage that have the greater chances of making it last. Jimmy encouraged, "When the life gets tough, hang in there with each other because going through it and getting over it together will make your marriage stronger after every bump. Will it be easy? No, not all the time, but it will be worth it in the end."

While the degree in which adversity hits varies from problem to problem, only through our dependency on God's grace and mercy can we deal and cope. Faith brings confidence and to remain in faith, we need coaching. Jimmy explained, "The ultimate goal in coaching is to become champions and having all the right components to achieve that goal and the tasks to keep athletes, parents, coaches, and a community all on the same page are demanding if not impossible when things like trophies are not won. So, when you or others are unsatisfied with your accomplishments or lack thereof, it is tempting to go the way of the world because it is during the down moments that your faith is really put to the test.

"As a Christian, you have the luxury of knowing that Jesus is always with you and that there will never be a problem that He cannot get you through. I know that He is the God of *all* things. When I need knowledge, wisdom, insight, or understanding, I turn to Him to provide it. Then, I relax because I know that I don't have to depend on myself. Trusting Him is the answer!"

One particular illusion that many people struggle with when it comes to the very suggestion of a relationship with God is that they think there is a need for them to be as sinless and pure as Jesus in order to be accepted and loved by God. This is not true. If we do not stop, learn, and correct this untruth, we will never let anyone get close to us, especially our hearts. The end results will always consist of failure and disappointment.

To God, sin is sin and He views it much differently than we do. Too many of us walk around holding onto grudges, hurt, anger, and the need to punish those who have wronged us. Jesus never did that. He died on the cross to cleanse the sins of all who accept Him and to remedy all the wrongdoings that have ever happened and ever will. If Jesus can ask God to forgive those who tortured and killed Him, shouldn't we forgive those who have hurt us?

As people, you must caution yourself in comparing your talents to others. Just as there are no two thumbprints alike, God also gave you individual and unique talents. Some gifts are easily seized and dispensed while others are more like buried treasures. Either way, grace and faithfulness are given to every one of us to some measure and you should nurture and develop your talents as you grow in your relationship with God. Use them to be a blessing to others.

Humanity as a whole, you are to exemplify Christ's characteristics as much as possible while on earth. Even if this sounds like an impossible task, you should make it your goal. Pray about it. Through prayer, true transformation can take place.

Jimmy prays all the time at no set schedule. Prayer is the conversation that he has with God just as if he were talking to a best friend. He knows when God is answering him because the answers involve an immense sense of love and help for others while receiving God's help for himself.

Words of Encouragement

"This world lives by a code of right and wrong. When we get caught for our wrongdoings, there are penalties such as time-outs, restrictions, fines, probations, or jail. God also operates by a code of right and wrong, and the many things He declares as 'sin' are wrong even by worldly standards.

"We will never escape death because we are a fallen species born into a fallen world; however, hell is something we can escape from. The escape is something perfect: belief and acceptance of Jesus Christ as our Lord and Savior.

"When Jesus came to earth, He lived a perfect and sinless life. His death on the cross was the only true perfect sacrifice for all compared to the Old Testament priests and Israelites who had so many rules and methods about sacrifices to attain forgiveness. Jesus paid the price for all sins, forever.

"When Jesus rose from the dead, He proved that He had power over death. When we accept this as truth, He sends His spirit into our hearts to live within us. It's a free gift to us that we can't pay for or earn. All we have to do is accept it and His love."

– **Jimmy Pate**

14

It is more blessed to give than to receive
(Acts 20:35)

"*The book of Acts is referred to as "The Acts of the Holy Spirit" because it focuses on the coming of the Spirit onto God's people in a new and powerful way. It records Christianity's amazing growth and shows that revival comes not by human effort, but by the power of the Holy Spirit, the same Spirit at work in your life today."* - Women's Devotional Bible.

As a kid, Steve Watson learned to act the right way, say the right things, and be respectful of others. He was genuinely a good kid who attended church regularly and at the age of 10, he accepted God into his life.

Regardless of how Steve survived adolescence and most indulgences, he occasionally stumbled in his walk with God. Nonetheless, his failures have never defined who he is, a child of God. Steve credits the extension of God's grace, conviction, and mercy for enabling him to eliminate bad habits, contemplate before establishing new ones, and correct his walk.

At the mention of faith and faithfulness, Steve pointed out why these can be difficult qualities to adhere to in our everyday settings. With a heavy heart, he said, "It's agonizingly simple. Old habits are hard to break. We are humans with tendencies geared toward selfishness. For example, when we smell an attractive aroma such as a favorite food, our first thought is to 'get some.' When someone comes to us for a favor, we think, 'What's in it for me?' Our mind spends a lot of time and effort in 'getting' – a job, necessities, creature comforts, or sex (pick your poison) – that we forget to be and to do what God wants of us so that He may bless us while we bless others. We deny His interest and investment in us to hold onto, grab at, and store up our riches instead being of service to our brothers, sisters, and especially Him."

In the summer of 2009, Steve and his family vacationed in Myrtle Beach, South Carolina. After a pleasant day with his family at the beach and shopping at various stores, they decided to indulge themselves with a seafood dinner at a local restaurant. Not thinking much about the name of the restaurant, their experience was an unforgettable one that he later regretted.

Seated inside, the staff placed paper hats on their heads as they did to all patrons without permitting them to know what was on them. The words written on his beautiful 15-year-old daughter's hat were: "Mom and Dad really think I'm not a slut! ... HA!"

While the restaurant environment was absolutely vulgar and offensive, Steve found the hats funny. So, they wore their hats, prayed over their meal, and enjoyed themselves with the rest of the lively restaurant patrons. A few minutes later, he noticed one particular family's reaction and response that truly exemplified moral goodness and God-ness - attributes he fell short of.

Seated next to them was a family with kids a little younger than Steve's. After scanning the room and then coming into full view of the words written on his daughter's hat, the couple whispered to each other, grabbed their kids, and exited the restaurant.

The observation brought a sense of clarity to what Steve should have done and the Holy Spirit's conviction upon his heart for ignoring the nudge from God that although he was required to live in this world, he did not have to be "of" it. Steve admitted that he should have made a better example of himself as a Christian, believer, father, and leader to his family.

Awareness of your sinful nature does not give you permission or approval to sin anyways. In other words, just because you are a believer in Christ and you walk in this world does not mean that you can go about your daily life doing whatever you want because you have faith. Do not take His forgiveness for granted! It is unfortunate, but our humanness often defaults us into temptations because they are constant, available, out of habit, and sometimes just plain hard to break away from. We always want things the easy way.

Knowledge in making the right choices and doing the right thing lies in the thought process of thinking to the end. Think of the possible consequences and ask yourself, "Is it worth it?"

Every person on this planet has a sense of right and wrong to some degree; however, it's the believer who sits in deep conviction and strives to improve their life, character, reputation, and walk in faith after succumbing to temptation. Steve encouraged, "Be aware that in battling your humanness, walking away from temptation and saying "no" can unfortunately leave you wanting and craving the temptation even more. Be ready for a fight within yourself!"

When we stay obedient in faith, the power of the Holy Spirit creates an overwhelming feel of satisfaction which is otherwise unattainable by worldly passions. Only a relationship with God can give you the strength and encouragement you need to achieve things you cannot do on your own. For Steve, he chooses God and a life of respect and value that honors Him.

His relationship with God has helped him have an improved perspective, opinion, and behavior toward women. He knows that the "ever-after" part is only possible in Heaven and that life "together" on earth has its struggles dealing with the daily grind and keeping sin from entering your lives and marriages. Steve warned, "If you look away from Jesus and outside your relationship with Him to attain true and genuine happiness, you're fooling yourself. Your struggles are going to be constant and will eventually cause havoc."

God's intention is not for your life to be filled with drudgery and anguish. He created you and the earth to be enjoyed while you live. So, see to each other's needs and desires within the framework of God desires for you and your spouse to enjoy one another. The only way for a husband and wife to attain these blessings with each other is to keep God at the forefront of their lives and union.

Just as God acknowledges Steve's needs, Steve acknowledges his wife's needs for provision, protection, respect, and decisions that all entail his selfless choices. Steve's attitude and actions toward his wife all fall in line with God's plan for their "man and woman" relationship because he makes the initiative to choose paths toward God's will. Steve stated, "A woman naturally feels the need for protection and provision from physical as well as emotional hurt. 'Let no man or woman interfere with what God has put together!' This command within itself explains the perfect balance when a man takes the initiative to pursue a woman and provide her with shelter, intimacy, appreciation, and attention."

If a man provides his wife with one of these qualities, but none of the others, their relationship will constantly struggle if not fail because there's no sense of trust.

The Holy Spirit has convicted Steve whenever his attitude, thoughts, or actions have been short of good and Godly ones. It was only after he had caught himself, stopped, and corrected his behavior that the Holy Spirit embraced him. In each instance, the embrace emanated an immense sense of love, peace, and satisfaction. With joy, Steve said, "When He pours His Spirit in, on, and around me, life is sweet!"

Stay focused on God and aware of His desire for a personal relationship with you. Keep yourself open, willing, and able to communicate, confront, and overcome the things that appear seemingly impossible, undesirable, and even challenging. This is faith and faith furnishes trust which bestows courage, strength, and honor regardless of what's happening in the world around you. With faith, you can stand firm and stand strong.

Practicing life through Jesus creates good habits in the same manner that sinning generates self-destruction. Quite a few people struggle with anger, patience, addiction, and discipline. Steve admitted that his biggest struggle is discipline, but encouraged, "Stop and think about what God would want you to do before choosing to act on impulse."

It is and has always been God who gives us the physical and mental strength to see beyond the setbacks of sin and walk onto the path of salvation. So, if you have stumbled, pick yourself up, dust yourself off, and try again! Your walk will improve, just watch.

Words of Encouragement

"This is God's desire for me, for you, and for everyone. If you are willingly open, inviting, and receiving of Him, I promise that the relationship is worth your time, effort, and life. You have nothing to lose and everything to gain. So, don't think that a life with God means leaving your comfortable surroundings to venture onto something else. The truth is: You will be moving forward onto bigger and better things than you could have ever imagined!"

– **Steve Watson**

15

Trust in the Lord with all your heart and lean not on your own understanding; in all your ways acknowledge Him and He shall direct your path

(Proverbs 3:5-6)

Faith and trust truly go hand in hand. One of the most concise definitions of faith found in the Bible is "... the assurance of things hoped for, certain of things not seen." (Hebrews 11:1)

Just like trust, faith means having the same level of confidence in, and reliance on, the virtues of integrity, strength, and the ability of another person or future fulfillment. However, when life gets difficult and things are not going your way, anchoring your mind and heart on these virtues can quite often, if not always, be as difficult as finding a needle in a hay stack. In other words, it can feel impossible, but when you take a step back from the situation burdening you and see the bigger picture, you will discover that God has proven Himself trustworthy on countless occasions. No matter the predicament, no matter the struggle, and no matter the pain, you can trust Him for a victorious outcome if you lean into Him. Once you remember and grab ahold of this truth, not only will your burdens lift, but your relationship with Him and others around you become easier.

Sam Botts is the second oldest of four children whom all grew up in the heart of Washington, D.C. During the era of Sam's childhood, his mother had two provisions in the tuition of him and his siblings. She wanted them to attain a good education and be schooled in a non-segregated environment. The only source of education around at that time to fulfill her wishes was private school under religious formation. So, for most of their education, Sam and his siblings attended Catholic school.

Unlike some who found faith in God late in life, Sam's faith was resolutely initiated, nurtured, and strengthened when he was very young. He credits this to his mother. Her repetitive exemplifications of kindness, respect, prayer, and obedience both in and out of their home were all instrumental in his established relationship with God through Jesus Christ. He asserts that the Bible is the handbook to life and that God's Word tells us how we are to behave, live, and act as humanity.

At the age of 15, Sam had a strong desire to become a priest. He attended a one week retreat at Oblates of Mary Immaculate in Newburg, New York to gain knowledge of the operation, treatment, and process to this calling. Although he was anxious to pursue the priestly path, he was encouraged by his family and church pastor to wait until after high school to make this decision.

During high school, his Physics class introduced him to the theory of "cause and effect" which confirmed and validated the existence of a higher being. The class also taught him that "matter" cannot be created nor destroyed and for every action, there is an opposite and equal reaction. Sam concluded that "matter" is "energy" and when it comes to our existence (everyone and everything living), there has to be a God because we did not appear out of thin air.

After high school, priesthood still weighed heavily on his mind, but it wasn't as strong as when he first felt it. He went about his life and got accepted into Howard University where his comprehension of God's existence increased.

Back home visiting from college, Sam and his brother went out one night to meet some friends for pizza. On their way back to their house, Sam's old tattered 1963 Volkswagen broke down. With nowhere to turn, they sat helpless in the middle of the roadway when the unfathomable happened: Two young white men around the same age as Sam and his brother pulled up next to them in a brand new convertible Corvette and asked if they needed help. These two men then got out of their car and helped push Sam's car to a safe location on the side road. Then, they squeezed Sam's brother into their car and drove him home so he could retrieve both his tools and another vehicle to go back and fix the broken down one.

For Sam, this incident of unconstrained kindness and assistance in an era where the cultural fabric of racism was at its peak in America affirmed God's favor, grace, and mercy. Regardless of the chaos in the world, good did exist.

After receiving his undergraduate degree, Sam continued onto law school where he met his wife, Linda, on a blind date. They have been married for over 40 years and have two grown children. Each child is a success in their own right and Linda is the president and CEO of a successful management consulting firm.

After law school, Sam joined the U.S. Navy as an attorney and was accepted into the Navy Judge Advocate Program as a Lieutenant Junior Grade

(LTJG). Before entering the Navy JAG Program, Sam had the pleasure of meeting the Judge Advocate General of the Navy. The Admiral was a kind, sincere, and committed man who clearly wanted to change the face of the JAG Corps. Sam learned that when the Admiral gave his word, the Admiral could be counted on to follow through with it.

The Admiral asked Sam where he wanted to be stationed and without putting too much thought into the answer, Sam replied, "California." The Admiral followed up with one condition: Sam had to attend and complete his education at The Naval Justice School. Sam agreed.

At the Newport, Rhode Island airport, Sam took a cab to the Naval Base. Upon his arrival, the cab driver told him the cost of his fare, $20. The smallest bill in Sam's pocket at the time was $50 to which the cab driver could not offer him change.

As Sam sat there wondering what to do, he spotted a Marine walking by. He quickly rolled down the window, pardoned himself, and asked him if he had change for a $50. Instead of supplying change, the Marine pulled out his wallet, asked the cab driver for the cost of the fare, and paid it. At the same time the Marine leaned in to pay the cab driver, Sam noticed that he was a Marine Captain: *A commissioned officer who has earned and accepted an appointment issued in the name of the president of the United States and who has the responsibility of leading Marines as they defend the Constitution of the United States.*

The next day, Sam reimbursed the Captain for his generosity and then never saw him again for the remainder of his stay at the base. This was yet another incident that further validated God's almighty power and grace of deliverance from another difficult situation. The lesson continuously learned has been God's justification.

Naval Justice School exceeded Sam's expectations. The Naval staff and Marines were respectful, kind, and hospitable to both Sam and Linda. They were invited to many social events as well as to their homes.

After Sam graduated in 1974, he was assigned to his first duty station in San Diego, California as promised by the Admiral. With their belongings packed, Sam drove his wife and their newborn son across the country to begin work as a Lieutenant Junior Grade (LTJG). A year later, he was promoted to Lieutenant. On record, Sam is documented as the third black Naval JAG Officer in the history of the Navy.

While stationed at the San Diego Naval Base, Sam made two long lasting friendships. His experiences with the military staff, Marines, and Officers of the Navy completely cemented his faith in God, his perseverance through the Holy Spirit, and his focus on the blessings bestowed upon him. He made use of them. Sam holds onto these beliefs and makes the best of everyday because His life and its predicaments all fall under the provision of God.

Through the power of God, Sam is protected at all times. For example, on three separate occasions, he has lost his wallet and has had it miraculously returned each time.

The first time Sam lost his wallet, he had been in a public place. Just as he was about to cross a street, a man came up behind him, tapped him on the shoulder and asked, "Did you lose this?"

When Sam looked down to see what the man gestured to give him, he saw that it was his wallet. Everything was still inside it.

The second time, he was in the parking garage of where he worked. He went looking for his wallet and could not find it. Just as he got on the phone to cancel his credit cards, a secretary from his office went to him and said, "Sam, the building engineer wants to see you."

Back inside the building, the engineer met Sam in the reception area. He said, "Mr. Botts, I believe you lost your wallet," and handed it to him. Again, everything was still inside.

The third time Sam lost his wallet, he and his family had been out shopping for a Christmas tree. After they selected a tree and returned home, they began decorating and planning their holiday when there was a knock at their front door.

At the door, a young man and his fiancé stood and asked for Sam. They informed him that they found his wallet lying in the parking lot of the Christmas tree kiosk. Clueless that he had even dropped it, Sam felt around and discovered that his wallet was missing. With wallet back in hands, Sam opened it and found his driver's license and all his credit cards in place.

Grateful and stunned at this young man's elaborate gesture in returning his wallet, Sam asked how they found his house. The man told him that he programmed his GPS with the address on Sam's license and he chose to physically return the wallet because he lost his wallet not long ago with much different results. He did not want someone else to endure the same inconveniences he did.

God prepares a person for triumph through experiences and circumstances that occasionally appear as unbearable obstacles.

In his younger years, Sam used to stutter. He stuttered so much that he couldn't pronounce vowels or the letters "t" and "s". This problem stayed with him into law school.

During his 26 years as a trial lawyer, someone once asked him why he chose to be a trial lawyer with a speech impediment. Wanting to provide an answer other than it was something he knew he had always wanted to do, Sam replied that whenever he was in trial and intensely focused on defending or prosecuting a case, he never stuttered. Those moments of intense focus brought clarity in speech. All Sam knew: *start of trial = no stutter and cross-examination = no stutter.*

Then, there was the time Sam's life came within inches of trauma, if not death. He had just left a lawyers' meeting in Baltimore City. When he stepped off the curb to cross the street, a car from down the street ran the traffic light and brushed past him. It missed hitting him by inches. Sam said, "The circumstances and events I've mentioned might seem trivial to someone else, but they have been huge for me."

Convinced beyond words that God's hand is always at work throughout our lives, this truth not only sweeps Sam off his feet, metaphorically speaking; but, reaffirms his faith in God over and over again. He declared, "There is a God and He does watch over us!"

While Sam remains comfortably nestled in the spiritual love, protection, and supply of God, he does not claim immunity to the adversities of life. He experiences good times and bad times just like you.

When surrounded by struggle, he leans on God and deeper in prayer than normal. Sam has said to God, "Lord, I know that You know what's going on, I know that You wouldn't send this to me if there wasn't a way out of it, and I know that You are trying to teach me something, but I'm a little slow. So, you're going to have to tell me what it is."

In those moments of prayer, Sam receives the help, strength, and encouragement he needs. In turn, he humbles himself before God all the while acknowledging the truth that humanity is nothing but dust without God.

Although there was a time in his life when he temporarily withdrew from church, Sam has never withdrawn from faith. Church has not only reaffirmed his belief, but it has provided and fulfilled his spiritual needs. He said, "God is always with me and He has been good to me and my family. God has even blessed me with things that that I had hoped for, but never asked."

As you know, adversity comes in all varieties and measures. They are the very difficulties that attempt to destroy your faith, break your heart, and test your integrity, sometimes with great success. While there are those of you who have conquered the clutches of temptation, there are those of you who have fallen entangled in the throes of making good and right decisions to walk away. When you are not careful, your strongholds can blind you to the consequences of your actions.

Admonishing temptation is not always an easy thing to do, especially after people have spent many years predominantly thinking of themselves and what feels good for the moment. Remember, Sam is a trial lawyer. He has seen and heard it all, so his assessment is professional as is real.

With respect, Sam explained the reasons behind some very concentrated strongholds which are responsible for many of the problems faced in society today:

Drinking and Drugs: "The reasons people drink or take drugs are vast and at times, unthinkable. What most don't realize is that these vices only numb their minds and provide a false sense of reality without ever fixing the problem. Alcohol and drugs give an unrealistic idea of present conditions, but most know the truth: Their 'problems' are still going to be there when they wake up and come out of their intoxicated and/or hallucinated condition. In the long run, they are harming their bodies by damaging their brain, liver, and other organs. What they need to do is think to the end and realize that the harm ultimately caused is to themselves and those whom love them."

Infidelity: "You may not hear about the poor choices made by a friend, family member, or neighbor, but they exist. Look at the news today. How many of our congressmen, senators, and people of high status have been unfaithful to their spouses? What about the wife suffering with cancer while the husband, for one moment of pleasure, destroys his family, his home, and his career? These are the consequences paid and suffered because he didn't think about what he was getting into. He did not think through to the end, or perhaps, he didn't care."

Dating: "Everyone yearns to share their lives with someone. It's a built-in yearning that God put within us so that the relationships we have with others mirror the relationship we have with Him. So, we go about dating hoping that 'Mr. or Ms. Right' find their way to us, and just when we think we've found them, we say to ourselves, 'This is the person I want to be with for the rest of my life.' To our detriment, our flesh is actually the one commencing this response. We 'feel' this way and make these gestures of love while knowing very little about our prospective partner.

"Consequently, these gestures usually lead to trouble because the flesh lies! Those who choose to live by the old saying, 'If it feels good, it must be good,' are in for a rude awakening! Life is going to knock them down! Just because it 'feels' good doesn't mean that it is good." As a trial lawyer, Sam has found it interesting when representing someone who knew they had done wrong. The moment these people hit rock bottom and finally acknowledged that they and they alone put themselves into a bad situation, Sam has heard some say, "Man! I have to get right with God."

is times like these that people come to God when all else fails. Sam stated, "Only God can keep you from making grave mistakes in life and only God can empower you to take a step back and think about making better choices."

As long as you fail to heed God's intervention and fail to listen to His guidance, your life will have more difficulties than not. The key to better days: You must seek Him, trust Him, obey Him, and most importantly, stop relying on yourself.

We all have different roles as men and women. The Bible tells us that "woman" is to be submissive to the husband and "man" is to respect his wife while he follows the Lord. The word "submit" is not meant as a gesture of servitude. A man is not to disrespect, degrade, or abuse the woman in his life or treat her as if she has no value. In any relationship, be it with God or a person, we must have a clear vision as to what we each want to do and as a couple, both of you are to look to each other for advice, opinions, and support. Cooperate with one another because men and women are equals and this is how God made us. Acknowledge and respect this fact or suffer because you are living by your own ideas.

When you are surrounded and engulfed with messages of wisdom from ungodly people, their advice and words usually consist of, "Suck it up," "Tough it out" or "This is the way of life, deal with it." Rarely do we hear people say, "Give it to God," "Let God handle it," or, "Go pray and seek His advice." The media has a great influence on how society perceives faith, marriage, loyalty, integrity, and adversity that make perseverance, patience, and forgiveness difficult. Sam explained, "For example, if you look at every old 1950 ᵃy film, you will notice that while the good guy ᵃⁱns, he never prays. Similarly, the action ₐay like James Bond, Spiderman, and Iron

Man to mention a few, they experience all kinds of danger and yet and again, they are victorious by their own efforts. They do not pray or even acknowledge God."

Words of Encouragement

"Unlike heroes of the media, God always provides you with another chance and is always with you. Look to Paul's Letter to the Galatians in all your conduct. 'But the fruit of the Spirit is love, joy, peace goodness, kindness, faithfulness, long suffering, gentleness and self-control' (Galatians 5:22).

"He tells you so in Scripture. On many occasions, God says, 'I am with you. I will not fail you or forsake you. Do not be afraid. Be of good courage.' (Joshua 1:6-9; Isaiah 41:10; Proverbs 3:25-26; Psalm 46:1; John14:27; Hebrews 13:5-6); and 'I will be with you until the end of age.' (Matthew 28:20)

"God is forgiving. All you have to do are two simple things: 'Trust and Obey Him.' (Proverbs 3:5)"

– **Samuel Botts**

16

Everything comes by faith

~~~~~~

The Bible firmly informs and encourages you to live every day for God, trusting Him in all things – especially your current circumstances – no matter how wonderful or dreadful.

Originally born in El Salvador, Elizabeth Evans is the second oldest of four children. Her parents successfully maintained a home environment centered on faith in Jesus Christ and because of this, their characteristics consistently portrayed Godly love, kindness, affection, respect, and honesty at all times, in all things, and to all people no matter what.

These attributes shaped Elizabeth's thoughts as a girl and through them the certainties of God were revealed to her as a woman. Only in Him does she find comfort and courage. Only in the Bible does she find answers, love, strength, and hope.

Aside from the emotional highs and lows of a typical girls' monthly menstrual cycle, Elizabeth's body intermittently produced ovarian cysts which triggered an irregular schedule and severe pain. At 14 years of age, she was informed by her doctor that her chances of having children later in life would be difficult because of this.

At 18 years of age, Elizabeth deeply believed she had life all figured out. Eager to break away from her parents, she moved out from their home, into her own apartment, and she ceased speaking to them for reasons she did not divulge. She quickly learned that in order for a person to "make it" in life, they must do everything they can to survive ... not an easy thing to do.

One day, she got notice that a very dear friend's father had passed away. As Elizabeth consoled her friend, he told her, "You know, for most of my life, my dad was a tough man – always demanding and pushing me hard with everything. Even though we would argue with one another almost every day, I loved him. Now, here we are. He's gone and I have to live the rest of my life knowing that I never told him. It's horrible. Don't ever do that with someone you really care about no matter how angry you might get with them."

Upon hearing these words, Elizabeth's pent-up resentment, hostility, and rebellion toward her parents dissolved. She excused herself and went to them. In a heartfelt state of humility, respect, and remorse, she apologized for her behavior and told them that she loved them. Just before their conversation ended, she humbly asked if she could visit them at their home. Her parents hugged her and her father replied, "Of course you can come to the house. That door has always been open."

While out in the world on her own, Elizabeth dated a young man for whom she fell quite hard for. As with most relationships, they experienced their good and bad days.

Her support system back then was her best friend, a girl whom she had known for many years. Elizabeth shared every joy, worry, complaint and disappointment she had with this girl, and, to her distress, she later learned that she also shared her boyfriend. Her "best friend" and "boyfriend" had been having an affair and the pains of infidelity and deceit weigh heavily upon her heart.

It took a long time for Elizabeth's heart to heal. Her disposition of heartbreak, depression, and cynicism were empathized by her family and friends. Her uncle actually made a personal attempt to snap her out of her it by setting her up on a blind date without her knowledge.

One morning, he phoned and told her to get dressed because he wanted to take her out for lunch. At the restaurant, her uncle informed her that a young man named Stephen who worked for him was supposed to join them. Elizabeth didn't mind because she thought he was just going to attend to some business while they ate.

Shortly after Stephen's arrival, her uncle stood up and announced that he had forgotten something so he had to leave, but he would be right back. Without much thought, Elizabeth and Stephen agreed to wait for his return. Twenty minutes later, she said to Stephen, "Well, it looks like he's not coming back anytime soon. Let's order some food." She and Stephen talked, ate, and laughed through their meal, and when it was over, Stephen drove her home because her uncle actually never returned.

Back home, Elizabeth walked in the front door, marched up to her uncle and complained, "How could you do that to me? Just leave me, your only niece, with a complete stranger?"

When her uncle got to work the next day, Stephen marched up to him and complained, "How could you do that to your niece? Just leave her with a complete stranger?"

Every day for the next several days following this, Stephen asked her uncle to have Elizabeth call him. Annoyed at his persistence, her uncle went to Elizabeth and insisted, "*Ei!* This boy won't leave me alone. Call him already! Call him and tell him that you care nothing for him and to stop bothering me."

That evening, Elizabeth phoned Stephen and to her surprise, her intended phone call to make Stephen go away generated into an hour long conversation and it was the most wonderful conversation she had ever had. After that, she and Stephen talked night after night and before long, they dated. A year later, they married.

For the longest time her uncle joked, "You weren't supposed to get married. I introduced you two to get you out of the house and have fun."

For you girls and women in the world who are hungry for love, Elizabeth advised with compassion and wisdom, "Regardless of career, goal, dream, and stance for independence as women, we're hungry for love and that forever-after guy just like every other female. We want someone who is respectful, honest, loyal, kind, and committed. We yearn for someone to want us as much as we want them and to share life with.

"These 'wants' pack honorable intentions while they also pack trouble if we're not careful. Why? Because quite often, our flesh wants to rush the game of courtship once we set our hearts on someone.

"This fearful, needy, and desperate approach – falsely labeled as tenacity, persistence, or power – results in our self-worth and self-respect being compromised. Besides, a man who has been pushed, pulled, pressed, or guilt-tripped into a relationship, usually has a ton of hidden baggage which remains blind to us until we are in so deep that it's hard to escape or set boundaries.

"God made a plan as to how we are to conduct ourselves as women and intimate partners when we are in a relationship. What gives couples the advantage in succeeding is being equally yoked in values, morals, and faith."

Do all women behave this way? No, but the unfortunate truth is that a good bit of them do. So, if you are already in the dating scene or venturing into it, keep in mind that everyone puts their best selves forward and that there is more to a person than what you see. Take your time, communicate, and do not compromise your deepest desires – especially if they come from a place of love – because, if the two of you are meant to be, you will have your entire lives with each other.

Just as Elizabeth stepped away from faith only to come back to it, our reasons for the same diversion vary. Elizabeth explained that her momentary lack of faith was due to a time of spiritual dryness, suffering, doubt, and her rebellion.

She has had several experiences with God. One in particular cemented her life to the life of Jesus Christ.

Shortly after marriage, Elizabeth and her husband had several conversations about their future and they agreed that two children were to be a part of it. Medical history aside, they hoped for a boy named Daniel and a girl named Ruth. They wrote their names on a piece of paper and tucked it away. Several years passed.

One day, while at work, Elizabeth sneezed and spotted her pants. At first, she presumed that she had started her period, but the bleeding quickly became excessive. She later learned that she had miscarried. She and her husband were devastated.

With optimism and purpose, Elizabeth and her husband strived to conceive immediately after. Months passed with no results. To improve and attain some kind of regularity and predictability in her bodily schedule, she began fertility treatments. A year later, she was pregnant.

The pregnancy initially went well, but eventually health issues developed. Elizabeth contracted diabetes and during her last trimester, she was put on bed rest because her uterus muscles could no longer hold the baby when she stood upright. Four months later, she delivered their son, Daniel. His name means, "God is my judge."

When Daniel reached eight months of age, Elizabeth and her husband decided that they were ready for another child. They also decided that because his conception was successful, the chances of another conception would be an easy one. Unfortunately, two years passed with no results and Elizabeth resumed the fertility treatments.

After several months, another treatment called *Basal Body Temperature*, a very useful tool that confirms a woman's ovulation was added to her regimen. Her day to day tasks of attention, medication, temperature taking, recording, charting, and scheduling took a psychological toll on both of them. The joy of lovemaking felt more like a job.

Three years passed before Elizabeth displayed pregnancy symptoms of morning sickness and severe mood swings. When she was tested, the results came back negative and then she was diagnosed with a rare medical condition called Pseudocyesis - in which a woman believes she is pregnant when she is not. Certain that her mind continued to play tricks on her, Elizabeth chose to ignore the symptom as they continued. However, once the morning sickness stopped, her body felt extremely different and she was retested. She tested positive. She was in fact pregnant. The first test result was a false negative.

Excited about the news, Elizabeth involved Daniel, then five-years-old, so that he could adjust and bond to the idea of being a big brother. He accompanied her to every exam.

Approximately two months into the pregnancy, Elizabeth miscarried. There was not as much physical pain during this particular miscarriage as there was stress in wondering why it happened and how her son would take the news.

Regardless of the disappointment, Elizabeth did not give up. She continued fertility treatments and after another two years had passed, she got pregnant. Now labeled a high risk, the doctor ordered more exams than usual as a safeguard and as an added precaution Elizabeth refrained from involving their son.

Into the second trimester, her fatigue and nausea completely ceased and her body started making room for the baby's growth. She started to wear maternity clothes and the baby's heartbeat always sounded strong. Elizabeth was healthier than she had ever been in her life and she made sure she got plenty of rest.

Regrettably, misfortune struck again. At her five-month exam, she lay on the examining table with the stethoscope to her belly. After several minutes, the doctor excused himself from the room and returned with two other doctors. Alarmed, but composed, she remained lying down as she watched and waited for one of them to say something as they took turns examining her. Finally, her primary obstetrician informed her that the baby's heartbeat could not be found.

Shock and confusion hit her like a brick. She thought to herself, "They have to be wrong. This can't be happening when I'm this far along." She phoned her husband, who met her at the hospital and after other tests were administered, it was confirmed that the fetus had expired. The hospital staff sent her home and told her to wait until her body discharged the fetus on its own. She carried that child for five grueling days in her protruding belly.

In her private moments, she begged God to tell her why while her family, friends, and church community all came to visit and pray over her. After the fifth day, the doctors admitted Elizabeth back into the hospital and surgically removed the fetus. The magnitude of this loss was shattering, but the message delivered to her son for the second time was the severest.

Elizabeth and her husband pulled themselves closer to God than ever before. Together, they prayed and expressed their feelings. They informed God that although they had originally desired two children, if one child was all that He had planned for them, they were more than satisfied. In agreement with her husband, they ceased all efforts to conceive both naturally and medically. Elizabeth said, "Through my three losses, the greatest lesson for me has been to appreciate and focus on what I have rather than on what I want. For this lesson, I was and still am grateful."

Elizabeth's struggles, triumphs, and catastrophes are reminders of how we all crave the upper hand in our circumstances, especially the unexpected ones. However, that is not how life works; instead, we experience let downs, blows, interruptions, and intrusions of the best and worst scenarios which can change the way we perceive life and even choose to live it. Life has taught her firsthand that the only way to receive help and any sense of comfort from such dilemmas is through faith. By depending and leaning on Jesus Christ, you can maintain the love, peace, and hope that can get so easily stripped away in your darkest hours. *When we let go, we let God.*

While getting on with her life completely at peace with no agenda other than nurturing their marriage, raising their son, and working, Elizabeth discovered that she was pregnant, again six months later during a regular physical.

As you can imagine, the news was not a joyous one. Fear consumed her and at that instant, she cried uncontrollably. Her mind raced with the thoughts, "Oh, no! Not again. I can't go through this again!"

Later that day, while home alone, she went to God in despair. She asked him, "Dear God, What do You want from me? Why this? Why now?"

Although it was an emotional and physical torment, 'acceptance' was the only thing that enabled Elizabeth to get through every hour of every day for herself and her family. Then, she was dealt a setback: A mass was discovered on the baby's head.

Initially, her doctor reacted professionally. Concerned that the mass was brain tissue, it was suggested that she abort the pregnancy immediately. Elizabeth refused. As the pregnancy progressed, her doctor's medical competence turned unprofessional.

The doctor told Elizabeth that she was selfish; that the baby would be born deaf, blind, or even paralyzed; and, both the medical care and bills alone would be beyond their capabilities. Then, the doctor said the unethical, "Bringing a child into the world with severe medical problems would embarrass their son."

Devastated by the doctor's unhindered remarks and manipulated attempts at guilt, all Elizabeth thought about was how she had not planned for this child. She declared, "Creation of life – no matter how wonderful, easy, lovable, unexpected, or devastating in its formation – is an act of God! I was not about to kill a life that God put in me. At least with this child, I would know why it was taken if I miscarried."

She immediately obtained a new obstetrician. One who was willing to remain professional, respectful, and considerate of her choices and faith while tending to her.

Exhausted by worry, Elizabeth experienced many sleepless nights and many nights in prayer. One evening, she prayed, "God, You gave me this child without me and my husband trying or even wanting it. If You want to take it, take it; otherwise, I am not going to end this baby's life just because it may not be how I want it to be."

At 1:35 p.m. on July 17, 2001, the medical staff packed the delivery room and Elizabeth gave birth to a thriving, crying, and kicking daughter baby girl. They named her Ruth, which means "friendship".

With Ruth in the intensive care unit for assessment and monitoring, Elizabeth was moved into a maternity room. Once settled, she petitioned to see Ruth, but the doctors denied her request. As she lay in bed for two days, heartbreak and anxiety weighed in on her as she listened to other bassinets with babies get wheeled past her room. . Every other mother in that maternity wing was bonding, nurturing, and loving their newborn, but her.

On day three, a nurse who was unaware of the circumstances and events of Ruth's delivery, showed up in Elizabeth's room for the morning shift. Again, Elizabeth asked to see her daughter. The nurse agreed to unite them as long as Elizabeth could prove she had her strength back. In response, she got out of bed, walked to the bathroom, took a shower, and got dressed.

Wheeled to the nursery, Elizabeth encountered Ruth hooked up to all kinds of monitors which made holding her, much less touching her, inaccessible. A little while later, Ruth was taken into surgery.

When the procedure was over, the surgeons returned to Elizabeth's room to inform her and Stephen of the results. The doctor's stated that surgery had gone well, but that they had good news and bad news to give them. Elizabeth and Stephen asked for the good news first.

The good news: Miraculously, the mass on the side of Ruth's head was not her brain, not attached to her brain, nor attached to any tendons inside her. The mass was an easily removed bulk of insignificant tissue.

The bad news: Ruth had a small hole in her skull which needed constant monitoring for swelling and leaking of spinal fluid while it healed. Other than that, she was a healthy strong baby girl.

Ruth was a medical miracle! The doctors said that they had never seen anything like this before in their lives. Medical history reports showed only one other similar case over 20 years earlier and that child did not survive.

Few words describe the emotions of relief and joy that flooded Elizabeth's heart. This experience in its entirety stretched every emotional and spiritual fiber within her beyond the boundaries of faith. God provided a special provision that sustained her with hope when all seemed impossible.

This past summer, Ruth turned 11 years old and she can do the same things any healthy kid her age can do.

Perhaps a person's faithlessness is due to the opinion that God has never done anything for them, or maybe they've suffered such great losses that they blame God for not protecting, healing, saving or intervening. While Elizabeth can sympathize with this view, it baffles her how a person can be so closed off to God's existence when there's so much evidence of Him around us.

Elizabeth said, "It doesn't matter if scientists do or don't prove that man evolved from a monkey or even a fish. God created that monkey and that fish. Look at the seasons. In early autumn, trees respond to the shortening of days and decline of sunlight which leads to the process of fall. You don't see human beings out in the woods or in their yards removing the leaves from the trees. God does it by providing wind that blows them off."

The day will come when we all meet our Maker. For those of you who are given "deteriorating days", you will most likely spend it with loved ones emotionally coming to terms with what awaits you. Some of you will become extremely fearful, maybe even desperate for God's face when you are at death's door while some of you will hold a sense of peace and satisfaction for your journey home. I ask you, "Why wait so long to look for Him? Why wait until your life is over when you could have been communing with Him the entire time?"

Elizabeth encouraged, "Don't wait until you are knocking at death's door for the truth to be revealed to you. You have a so many chances for God to touch on something in your life. To experience Him, you must be open and inviting to Him because God never pushes, presses, or forces Himself upon anyone."

For the believers who balance themselves on the fence of faith, be ready for the rude awakening that believing is not enough to attain you a seat in Heaven! You do not have to attend church every Sunday, but consistent worship with others is good for the soul, and prayer, in a group, is far more powerful than prayer alone. Try it and see what mountains move.

Sunday church services for Elizabeth and her family go beyond the average hour or two like most other religious services. While the attendees come together under one roof for the pastor's message, both praising and fellowship feel more like a family reunion. As brothers and sisters in Christ, they pray with one another and for one another, they share meals, attend to whoever needs help, and nurture each other's walk in faith with the uncomfortable task of accountability - which is good for their growth.

God exemplifies His mercy and grace in Elizabeth's life and in her family every day. His will and power stand out loud and firm.

Many years ago, Elizabeth's father suffered a severe heart attack. While waiting for him to stabilize, he suffered three more heart attacks that caused him to slip into a coma. While he slept, countless people from their church and community visited and prayed over him. Three days passed with him in this state comatose.

On Mother's Day, Elizabeth's mother received a call from the hospital. The doctors petitioned her and the family to visit as soon as possible because his vital signs weakened and he was not expected to survive the night.

With the family at his side, they all took turns speaking to him. When her mother leaned in and quietly spoke words of love into his ear, the power of God revealed itself to everyone in the room. His vital signs strengthened, his eyes opened and he gestured for a pen and paper to write on. When handed these items, he wrote, and when he turned that paper around, it read, "Happy Mother's Day."

In total amazement, Elizabeth asked, "How can a person be so sick that they lapse into a coma for days, yet still have the brain function to know what day it is when they wake up? How can a person be so close to death and, in a second, be here? There wasn't a calendar in my father's room. There is no explanation other than God!"

The most recent circumstance that revealed God's mercy, grace, power, and healing to her again, also brought her husband to the feet of Jesus.

December 2011. Just days before Christmas, Elizabeth, her children, and parents were getting ready to leave for a meeting at their church regarding Christmas festivities while her husband, Stephen, also got ready to leave for a client's house so he could finish working their roof. As they were all walking out the door, Elizabeth reminded him of his promise to attend the meeting with them and he reassured her that he would be there as soon as he was done.

Around noon, Elizabeth phoned Stephen to remind him to watch his time, and again, Stephen reassured her that he would be there.

Hours passed and a little after five o'clock that evening, Elizabeth's phone rang. It was the homeowner where Stephen had been working. The woman said, "Mrs. Evans? I am calling to let you know that there has been an accident with your husband. You need to get to the hospital immediately."

After getting the details of her husband's accident and whereabouts, Elizabeth went to the hospital as quickly as she could. Her parents stayed behind with their children.

When she first arrived at the hospital, the receptionist could not find him. A few minutes later, he was located under the alias name, Sunset - a code name that all trauma patients receive when their vitals turn life threatening while being transported. Elizabeth made her way to him.

His injuries were tremendous. In fact, Stephen looked like he had been hit by a train. After falling 30 feet from the client's rooftop and having landed on his side, his pelvic bones were shattered. On impact, they ripped into his organs and caused internal bleeding.

The doctors did everything they could to save his life. Swollen, discolored, bandaged and hooked to machines with tubes running everywhere, Elizabeth's world, as well as Stephen's, came to a halt. She phoned her parents and had them bring their children to the hospital. Once they were altogether, their prayers as a family commenced as did word of his accident to their extended families, friends, church, and community. Prayers were abundant!

In times of surrender, Elizabeth deeply reflected on their marriage. The memories baring the most concentration were the times she felt irritated and angry with him. Afterward, she made a very personal plea to God. She said, "Dear God, please don't take Stephen. I know that I've complained at times, but please don't take him, not yet. I'll be a better wife. One that encourages and guides him lovingly and unconditionally to be the man You created him to be. Just please don't take him."

Elizabeth always believed that she knew what love was, but when this possibility of losing Stephen was presented, the meaning, depth, and strength of love took on a whole new perspective. In January 2012, Stephen was taken off life support. Since then, he has learned to walk and now has feelings in areas of his body that were once numb.

The one practice of faith repeatedly exhibited by Elizabeth throughout her life has been prayer. She affirmed that the only requirement in effective praying is honesty. Talk to God just like you would a friend. Whisper to Him, plead to Him, cry to Him, and even yell to Him if you feel the need. Keep your conversations real and then feel His love sweep over you. That is faith, you in God and God in you.

As God's children and humanity as a whole, we are to be unselfish to and helpful of others in all that we do. You are to be kind, generous, and most of all, non-judgmental.

Words of Encouragement

"Without God, you're going to keep doing what you have been doing and you're going to keep experiencing what you have been experiencing. Without God, your life – your soul – is not going to improve. Invite Him in and discover the one thing that can fill in all the empty spaces within your heart."

– Elizabeth "Febe" Evans

17

God is good in both His love and justice

Mother Theresa once said, "The greatest gift a parent can give a child is unconditional love. As a child wanders, strays, and searches for his bearings, he needs a sense of absolute love from a parent. There is nothing wrong with tough love, as long as the love is unconditional."

Brad Clark is the oldest of three. As children, they were close and as adults, they remain that way today. Regardless of the miles between them, they get together for Easter, Thanksgiving, Christmas, and each of their children's birthdays.

Due to his father's time in the Service, he and his family got to travel quite extensively. From the west and east coasts of the United States to the streets of West Germany, Brad was exposed to a diverse amount of cultural lifestyles. Every person, place, and thing was a unique and wonderful experience no matter how uneasy he initially felt after each move.

As a kid, Brad Clark enjoyed collecting coins, searching for buried valuables, reading books, watching movies, and accumulating anything and everything he could that had to do with pirates.

As a teenager, his hobbies turned to music. The sounds of hard rock and heavy metal music fashioned a desire to play the guitar and before long, he could play classical music on an acoustic and heavy metal music on an electric.

In the course of his adolescence, a couple of momentous incidents occurred that could have – and perhaps, should have – caused Brad great harm or even death.

At the age of 10, Brad and a friend were walking down a street on their way to a store. Just as he was crossing the street, a car sped past them and clipped Brad in the leg. The force of the impact spun him into the street and to the ground. By the time the driver stopped, got out, and inquired if he was okay, Brad stood up, reacted as if nothing had happened, and said that that he was fine. The driver left and Brad limped away in severe pain.

The other time was when Brad was in his late teens. He had gone to a party and got drunk. When the evening was over and he was ready to leave, he decided to drive home. Luckily, as he sat in his car, he was very aware of his inebriation before driving off. Minutes later, he received an impression to make himself sick in an attempt to lessen his drunkenness. He leaned out the door, stuck his finger down his throat, and vomited. A few minutes later, he felt sober and drove home.

Divine protection must have been over him because his state of 'lucidity' only lasted for the duration of his drive home and not a minute more. Back in his parent's driveway, intoxication flooded back over him. He stumbled his way into the house, crawled into bed, and slept it off.

No matter how capable or competent a person appears in their faith, every one of us has experienced a fall from faith at some point in time and this holds true for Brad, such as when he lost his temper with his brother. This must have happened one too many times because Brad eventually gave up on being a Christian altogether. That is, until the age of 20, when he experienced a powerful intercession that transformed and fastened his life to God's existence.

Living with his parents, Brad had been feeling extremely depressed. While he listened to music on a record player in his room, he felt and then heard a very distinct voice instruct him to get rid of the music so he could be helped. Without hesitation, Brad reached for an old Civil War bayonet and smashed the record player until it stopped playing. After he put the bayonet down, he walked out of his bedroom in a state shock at what he just heard and witnessed himself do. When his mother saw him walk past, she asked him if he wanted to go to church with her. Brad replied, yes and an hour later, to church they went.

Back home and in his room, Brad walked up to the record player to examine it when he noticed a picture of Jesus and a sailor in an oval wooden frame. In the photo, Jesus had one hand on the sailor while His other hand pointed the way for the ship to be steered. As he examined the photo more meticulously, he noticed two very inquisitive things: There was a small nick in the paper just over Jesus' heart and there was a small round protrusion in one corner of Jesus' mouth.

At first, he fathomed that a piece or two of the record player must have rocketed across the room and put those defects in the photo when he was in his smashing frenzy. Then, he heard that same distinct voice that he heard earlier in the day speak to him again. Brad was told that it was He, Jesus. Jesus told him that He loved him and that his earlier actions of listening and obeying touched His heart. Overcome with immense love and adoration for Him, Brad knew that he had just witnessed a miracle with his own ears and eyes. As he cried, all of his pent up feelings of loneliness and sadness were released. The truth had set him free.

Brad's focus in life soon turned away from his own wants and needs to the wants and needs of others. It was as if God poured His love for all mankind out and through Brad and to this day, Brad feels God's mercy, grace, and peace. Whenever he has moments of sinning or falling short of God's will for his life, the peace he feels is instantly replaced with guilt; however, when Brad holds himself accountable through confession and seeking forgiveness, God's peace and benevolence return to him.

Brad moved to Springfield, Missouri when he was 22 years old to attend Bible College. While there, he met his wife, Cindy. Cindy is also a Christian and after he graduated, they married. The relationship they each have with Christ is the model relationship they have in their marriage with each other.

Their marriage is strong because God is at the center of it and this threefold cord is not easily broken. When problems arise, Brad and Cindy take them to the Lord together in prayer. That is when their mountains of adversity move out of their way.

Brad's choice to follow Christ has helped him have a higher quality of life on this side of death. Christ guarantees that the highest quality of life is waiting for him in eternity after his death and this holy attraction to God is progressive in nature and personal reflection through Bible study and prayer.

Prayer, Bible study, fasting, and reading spiritually encompassed materials, such as *The Practice of the Presence of God* by Brother Lawrence, *Abandonment to Divine Providence* by Jean-Pierre de Caussade and a *Testament of Devotion* by Thomas Kelly, best encourage faith. Brad attests that when these particular exercises of faith are practiced simultaneously, not only are worldly strongholds demolished, but big breakthroughs, blessings, and rewards of all kinds occur. The greatest reward for Brad is and has always been a sense of refreshed faith. His relationship with God becomes even more enriched with greater devotion, intimacy, respect, and love - all of which attract quality (not quantity) friendships. These sorts of friends listen and when asked, encourage Brad to stand back from situations for just a moment and become more observant of what is right and what is wrong while never abandoning him. They enhance Brad's integrity, morals, and loyalty to God and himself along with his wife, children, family, friends, work, and obligations.

Brad encouraged, "As a believer of Christ, practice the presence of God in every moment, especially in times of severe hardship because it's in those moments where God is found. Become aware to that still small voice of the Holy Spirit that gently guides you in your daily walk. When you let Him take care of what is out of your control, you find the peace your heart aches for."

As you know by now, a relationship with Christ does not keep you immune to various difficulties of life here on earth; however, it can keep you from falling apart spiritually, emotionally, and intellectually when fastened and applied.

Brad's faith has been tested. He stated, "During the first couples of years into my marriage, I went through a difficult time with my job in Kentucky. I had a bad supervisor who created unnecessary stress in my life. Thankfully, God blessed me with a Christian lady who was my supervisor's supervisor. This lady, higher in the chain of command, helped me get a promotion which resulted in my move back to northern Virginia. At my going-away party, I never retaliated; instead, I publicly thanked my supervisor for her assistance. My actions of unconditional regard and kindness not only surprised her but, surprised my co-workers because they felt a reprisal from me was due and justified. The scenario in its entirety was proof to both me and my wife that God is always with us."

Awareness of this truth brings confidence in all that Brad thinks, feels, says, and does. Amid times of financial struggle, he and his wife trusted God while they changed their spending habits. While recuperating from surgery, Brad realized and then contemplated on just how truly fragile the human body is while relying on God's healing process. Then, the greatest challenge came in 2008. Their son was diagnosed with Tourette's syndrome. Through prayer, Brad and Cindy obtained one of God's attributes: patience.

These situations and many more conclude that when you seek God's help in mastering a struggle in your life, He presents you with situations that transform that struggle into strength.

Brad strives to learn from his experiences, as well as the experiences of others and what the Scriptures say will have bad consequences. A recent revelation came when Brad contemplated on God's relationship to all the inequities in the world, including the disabilities and ugliness that some people suffer. God revealed that these inequities are in fact His. Not that He causes them, we do that on our own, but He shares in their pain with love.

Words of Encouragement

"There's an importance to being sincere and living consistently with one's conscience. Keeping this in mind will point you to God as your moral source. In the Bible, God revealed that He will forgive those of us who sin against Him and that Jesus is the very origin of His forgiveness. Jesus paid for all our sins by taking on the penalty of death, the punishment we all deserve.

"His resurrection promises that when you trust in Him, His Spirit will come to reside within you. Through the Holy Spirit, you will be lead according to the calling that He has given you which will not only fulfill the desires of your heart, but will enable you to live joyfully and peacefully forever with Him."

– **Brad Clark**

18

*There is a time for everything,
and a time for every purpose
under the Heavens*
(Ecclesiastes 3:1)

~~~

Fate, destiny, and luck – forces that seem to operate for the good or ill of your life through events, circumstances, and opportunities. Life is an ongoing process, a gradual growth in grace, unfolding in every surrounding, situation, and choice that changes from season to season.

Just as life is in motion, so is God. He is always moving toward you and working with you wherever you are as you are. As you learn to trust in His power, His light shines into the darkest hours and the darkest hearts so, never say, "What's the use now? My life is half over." When you realize that what God has for you and accept the fact that only He can untangle your messes, He will prove Himself worthy as you yield yourself and allow Him to lead the way.

Miles Galicia, the youngest of two, was originally born and raised in the Philippines. Her friends are quick to tell you that she is a woman of great love and admiration. Her characteristics of respect, humility, service, compassion, self-discipline, patience, ethical, honesty, forgiveness, diplomacy, leadership, and loyalty have affectionately earned her the nickname "Jedi." She makes herself available to listen and to be leaned on by everyone unless life circumstances hinder her availability. She wears her heart on her sleeve – an attribute that many fear and fail to reveal nowadays.

Miles and her older sister have always been very close. Her father worked as an overseas foreign worker which unfortunately kept his presence and availability scarce. He was hardly ever home. As for her mother, she abandoned the family when Miles and her sister were very young. Could their father's absence have prompted their mother's departure? Maybe, but her reason for leaving has remained unexplained even to this day.

Miles and her sister were raised by their grandparents, the family matriarch and patriarch. Although their parents were not around, the parental structures of love, support, money, wisdom, and discipline were provided, as was religious encouragement.

After every Sunday service, their grandma took them to a local candy shop where American candy was sold and they were each permitted to choose one bag, roll, or box of whatever they wanted. Miles and her sister would sit quietly and divide their candy with one another to the rhythmic tune, "One for me and one for you." Whenever there was an odd amount of colors or pieces left over, they gave them to their grandma. Aside from this tidbit of affectionate bonding, there were no special treatments given or displayed toward Miles and her sister just because their parentless situation.

As Miles dug into the memories of her past, she stated that her mother's actions of running off and eloping with another man brought shame and dishonor to the entire family. In turn, her 'extended family' of aunts, uncles, and cousins responded with behaviors of resentment and animosity toward both her and her sister. She said, "We felt hated by everyone, except our grandparents."

When her grandfather was dying, her 'extended family' expected Miles and her sister to be returned to their father; but, before he drew his last breathe, he announced to everyone that neither of them would be moving out of the only home they had ever known as long as he or his wife were alive. Following this declaration, moral poison of jealousy and hatred ran through the hearts and minds of 'extended family' and whenever an opportunity to harm Miles or her sister presented itself, they acted on it.

For instance, one time, Miles accidentally spilled something and her uncle severely beat her with a leather slipper. These so-called "close relatives" knew that these girls had nothing and never, not once, did they ever extend or express any kind of compassion or kindness to them to alleviate the pain of abandonment or rejection they had been feeling from the start.

Just as her eyes are brown and her hair is dark, I believe the attribute of 'perseverance' is also built into Mile's DNA. She revealed this quality when she said, "Due to the abuse dealt out by my extended family, I developed an attitude of, 'I don't care how anyone treats me. I'm doing my best because I'm doing it for my Grandma.'"

Her father did whatever he could whenever he could. He gave her grandparents, his in-laws, as much financial support as possible. His monies combined with theirs helped Miles and her sister attain an education at a private parochial school with the rest of their family cousins.

Miles loved school and when she was not in class, she pursued every school activity she could get involved in. As for school uniforms, the girls made due with 'hand-me-downs' from strangers and neighbors. Regardless of the clothing's wear and tear, their grandmother made sure they looked presentable for school every day. At a class reunion, some childhood classmates commented to Miles, "Your school uniform may have been old and faded, but it was always nicely pressed."

Miles dated a boy through high school and into college. She believed that they would marry one day because quite often, they had conversations about their future together. They made plans and they saved money. Sadly, the boy stopped seeing her shortly after she started to work. Miles stated, "He literally disappeared from my life one day. He never gave me an explanation and it caused me great heartache."

In need of comfort from the break-up, solace came from a man enduring a divorce. The more time he and Miles spent together, the more attracted they became to one another. Eventually, one thing eventually led to another and before she knew it, Miles discovered that she was pregnant.

Confusion and shame bombarded her mind at the idea of being a single mother much less a single pregnant woman. To cope, she spent a lot of time in a small chapel on the college grounds between her work and classes contemplating her situation. Almost every day, she went to pray, give thanks, give praise, find guidance, and feel connected to God. Those visits of solidarity calmed her worries every time. Church was where her heart found peace and where she communed with the One who always lifted her up. In her heart, she knew that in order for Him to help her, she had to take responsibility for her predicament. So, with humility and accountability, she asked Him for His forgiveness and then expressed to Him both her pains and fears. Soon afterward, God responded.

Miles received a new job with more money that enabled her to live on her own. To shield herself from her family's potential condemnation, finger pointing, and disappointment, she told a 'white-lie'. She told her grandmother that her new job required her to relocate far away so, she had to move out. She referred to this time of secrecy in her life as "the dark days" because she had no idea what each day had in store for her.

In the course of her fears, she never visited her family or experienced the misfortune of running into anyone who could run back and gossip. The few friends she kept near her all believed that God was truly watching over her.

Miles worked hard, lived quietly, and several months later, delivered her daughter, Kristine. Her supervisor, who became a strong father figure to her, and his wife, supported, assisted, and treated Miles as if she were a part of their family. On a fast track, they rewarded her with promotions and pay increases. One afternoon, she was called into his office. He advised and encouraged her to go back home and share her newborn daughter with her family. At first she hesitated, but later agreed. When she expressed her concerns about breaking the news, he informed her that he had already done it. Weeks earlier, he had visited her grandmother and informed her of Mile's life.

The following weekend, Miles visited her grandmother. After Kristine was introduced to her entire family, no one said much. Miles credited their silence to two reasons: One - she never asked for help from anyone; and two - she was financially successful in her own right.

Eventually, Miles met a man and married. He was kind and he embraced her daughter Kristine as if she were his own. In the course of their marriage, they moved to the United States of America and brought two more children, Raimond and Jessi, into being.

The way to open up, change, and nurture your relationship with God is through prayer. Miles encouraged, "Never tire out of praying even if it means praying for the same things over and over again. Going to God and petitioning Him can sometimes be compared to the likes of sitting in a waiting room at a doctor's office. There are some people around you with more severe conditions than yours, and although their diagnosis and treatment is a priority, your turn will soon come so, remain patient. As you wait, do something of value and good with your life in the meantime. Don't just sit there and wait for God to respond."

In the course of this journey called "life," you may take the wrong road or you may have a detour, but God will always provide you endless opportunities to correct your course. Therefore, wake up each morning in thankfulness. Thank God for another day, implore Him to guide your decisions, and ask Him to help you think, act, and speak in ways that please and honor Him.

Words of Encouragement

*"Be not afraid , I go before you always
 Come follow me and I shall give you rest."*

"The will of God never takes you where the grace of God won't protect you.' If you have faith in this phrase, rid your fears and imagine what you'll learn, accomplish, change, and feel if you're not afraid of failure, breakthroughs, love, and the truth."

– **Miles Galicia**

19

A man of disbelief is at the mercy of a man with a testimony

About the Author

~~~

Sometimes words of skepticism, disbelief, and debate from those who strive to dispute the very existence of God can sound quite convincing, but when we are quick, sound and gentle in explaining our reasons for hope in God, nothing – and I mean "no person, place, or thing" – encompasses the authority to erode or eradicate the power behind and within our faith.

Born in 1966, I am the youngest of three children raised in a middle-class home in Landover Hills, a small town in Maryland. My father was a car salesman and my mother was a legal secretary at the county courthouse. Together, they made life very comfortable for all of us; but eventually, just like so many of their friends, their marriage succumbed to divorce.

While the feel of 'home' was lost, I lived between the two of them almost on an annual basis for the next several years. Despite my efforts and theirs, my craving for consistency, structure, permanency, and protection were never satisfied.

As for religion, our family attended church every Sunday morning. Although I never found church enjoyable as a kid, there was one thing that made our attendance seem all worthwhile. Every Sunday when services were over, my parents took us to the local bakery for our choice of any fresh baked donut. These servings of "holy donuts" were my taste of Heaven.

After careful contemplation on the day-to-day exemplifications of others, I truly believed that belief in God was all I needed, never mind being obedient or making it personal. I witnessed family and friends confess on Wednesdays, worship on Sundays, and go back to acting like devils on Mondays and they were satisfied with their lives.

Following graduation in 1984, I worked as a clerk at the same courthouse as my mother. This was where I met my husband, a correctional officer at the county jail, across the street. We married in October 1987 and three months later, I gave birth to our oldest child, David. Within the following nine years, I delivered two more children, another son and then, a daughter. My children are my greatest accomplishments in life.

The Bible states that the enemy comes to steal, destroy, and kill. Well, Satan must have had a field day in my marriage because it eventually crumbled and robbed my children from full-time parents, their home, stability, security, holidays together, and family dinners. I still have moments where I wonder if I knew then what I know now, perhaps the enemies of abuse, neglect, greed, selfishness, lies, alcohol, drugs, and adultery that invaded our marriage, on both our parts, would have been properly drop kicked out and into the universe. Unfortunately, neither one of us were properly adjoined to God or godly living during those years.

Growing up, I went through many phases of personally testing my life boundaries and limits. I have lied to stay out of trouble, stolen to see what I could get away with, cursed to sound like an adult, smoked to appear cool, and drank to be part of the crowd. I did what most typical teenagers do, but thankfully, God caught my attention over the next decade with several intense interruptions where there were no explanations other than a divine one.

A Godly reality: When I was seven years old, I tagged along with my mother to confession one evening. Inside, the church was dimly lit – as most Catholic Churches are – and people were lined up one behind the other in several areas. One by one, they entered a room not much larger than a closet. I had no idea what was waiting on the other side of that door but whenever the person who went in re-emerged, humility was all over their face. They would then walk into a pew, kneel, bow, and pray.

When it was my mother's turn to go in, she grabbed me, walked in, and knelt on a kneeler that faced a wall with a small mesh window face level. Once the door closed behind us, the room was pitch black. Off in the background, I faintly heard a man speaking. A few seconds later, that small window in front of my mother slid open with an abrupt thud. Intense fear ran through me. A shadowed silhouette of a man's profile appeared. In a deep masculine voice, he said, "Good evening, my child. What is it that you have come to confess?"

I had no idea who he was, but I almost fainted because my mind assumed it was God up close and in my face. Latched onto my mother, I whispered, "Is that God?" She never replied. She just wrapped her arm around me and pulled me close for reassurance.

When their conversation was over, my mother grabbed my hand and lead me back out into the church. Into a pew, I watched her do exactly what I had seen everyone else do, she knelt, bowed, and prayed. It was years later that I learned that this was the pattern for the Act of Contrition.

The power of prayer: When I was seven months pregnant with my daughter, I went to my obstetrician for my monthly exam. My doctor and I had a good rapport with one another, so he would administer a Doppler ultrasound test for my sheer enjoyment.

With the Doppler device on my belly, he couldn't locate a sound. At first, neither one of us gave the silence much thought because we both figured that he just needed to find the right spot. After several unsuccessful attempts of finding the babies heartbeat, he put the Doppler headphones onto his ears, closed his eyes, and placed all of his senses into the test. As I stared at him waiting for an expression of *"Aha!"* to come over his face, I got nothing. A few seconds later, he opened his eyes, removed the headphones, and softly asked, "When was the last time you felt the baby move?"

Honestly, I couldn't answer him because I hadn't been paying attention. My days were so busy keeping house and raising two boys that I truly had not paid attention. He scheduled me a return exam a week later.

With a sympathetic hug goodbye, he said, "Perhaps, the baby is just hiding today. Remain calm and in the meantime, pay attention to any kind of movement. I'll see you next week."

Back in my car, I phoned my husband. My composure crumbled as soon as I heard his voice. Words of any kind couldn't and wouldn't sound out over my tears. I forced myself to take a deep breath and hysterically blurted out what happened. He was as shocked as I was.

My usual 20-minute drive home took over an hour because I had to pull to the side of the road several times to wipe the tears that caused me to be a serious road hazard. Once home and settled into my routine as 'mom' to my boys, I phoned my mother to give her the news. She reminded me to have faith. It was a nice reminder, but not something that I truly leaned into, not until a few days later.

1st Sign – an elder's help: A few days later, my mother phoned me with a simple yet implausible request. She instructed me to ask for the added prayer of Saint Gerard, the Patron Saint of Pregnant Women, as I prayed to God. I was to request St. Gerard's added petition to mine three times a day for three days and after the third day, I was to look for the symbol of a rose because it represented answered prayer. The "rose" could be of any color or quantity, be given to me or to someone else, or show up as a simple picture in a magazine or television ad. With nothing to lose, I began the triage of prayers the next morning. Then, on day four – Sunday, December 15, 1996 – God's mercy and grace emerged.

I made breakfast for my 'guys' then shuffled my boys off to church with me. Half-way through the service, just when the Eucharist was being brought to the front of the church, I looked up and noticed a woman holding a vase with a dozen red roses. She placed them on a podium in front of us. When I looked around, another woman placed a dozen white roses on a podium on the other side of the church. At first, my mind was consumed with the oddity of roses in the middle of winter. Then, the symbolic message behind those roses sank in.

The prayers worked! I was told what to do and what to look for as a sign of answered prayer and it happened. The torments of fear and worry that had a hold on me, lost their grip.

The following Wednesday, I was back at my doctor's office for the follow-up exam. This time, when the Doppler test was administered, the strong, loud, repetitive rhythms of a heartbeat – as sweet as church bells – sounded. Two months later, my daughter graced us with her presence. She weighed in at 6 pounds, 8 ounces and she was healthy.
     This was the beginning of faith; I started to get acquainted with Christ. He progressively nurtured my soul and life into something far more glorious than I could have ever anticipated, but before my life improved and I became obedient, I still struggled with separating myself from this world.
     2nd Sign – His power: When I left my marriage, I relocated to Florida with my two youngest children. On July 4, 2001, my son had gone outside to light sparklers with my dad. Within minutes, they both came running into the house in a panic. Danny was in tears and holding his hand. My dad said, "Hurry, get some ice! His hand is burnt."
     There were second degree burns on the palm of his hand and several fingers. Immediate blistering occurred. I was advised not to take him to the hospital because fireworks of any kind were illegal and social services would be called. That meant my son would more than likely be taken from me even though I didn't provide the sparklers.
     Intense fear ran through my mind. I searched my dad's hall pantry and found a jar of Silvadene, a topical burn ointment. I swabbed Danny's hand, wrapped it in gauze, covered it with a latex glove to protect it from washing off and then, stuck it in a bowl of ice water.
     At bedtime, Danny was pumped up on Tylenol and put to bed on the sofa so that his hand could lay over the side and into the bowl. He fell asleep, but at 2:00 a.m., he woke me up in severe pain. I was at a

loss on what to do. I couldn't give him anymore pain medication because enough time hadn't passed yet. As my mind raced with ideas of what to do to comfort him, I heard a voice say, "Pray for him." I told Danny, "I don't know why I'm being compelled to do this, but give me your hand."

With his injured hand in mine, I silently prayed to God and Archangel Raphael (whose name means God's healing) to grace Danny with healing and comfort. In the midst of this prayer, Danny jerked his hand out and away from mine. When I opened my eyes to discover the reason for his retraction, his eyes were as big as saucers. I asked, "What happened?" Danny replied, "I don't hurt anymore, Ma'. My hand, it feels fine."

With hope and optimism, I finished praying. Danny fell back to sleep and remained asleep the remainder of the night.

In the morning, my father and I removed the bandage from Danny's hand and to our complete amazement, not a blister, blemish, or mark was on him. His hand was completely healed.

The storm: Three months later, Danny approached me and tearfully expressed his desire to move back to Maryland with his father and brother. A week later, I packed his belongings and drove him to his father's. Our daughter, who was only 3 years old, remained with me in Florida.

When I sent my daughter to her father's for a Christmas visit, he informed me that she was staying with him on the day of her scheduled return. With our signed agreement in hand and a certified letter from the local sheriff, I retrieved my daughter.

My family warned me not to send her for another visit. They believed that my estranged husband would attempt to keep her again and it would end with very different results. Although I knew that their concerns were legitimate ones, my conscience wouldn't provoke me to deliberately eliminate him from her life. I may not have gotten along with him, but he was her dad and they loved each other as much as she and I loved each other; besides, her brothers were living in Maryland as well.

Easter 2002 - I sent Laura to him another visit. Everything I was warned about manifested. Unbeknownst to me, my estranged husband had retained an attorney and filed papers falsely stating that all three of our children were residing with him, that I abandoned our home, and that I was threatening to remove one, if not all of them. The judge was unaware of our signed and notarized separation agreement. Not knowing any different, the judge granted him full physical custody of all our children pending the divorce - a two year ordeal.

Rock bottom: I phoned my children as I did every night only to hear the operator's voice say, "This line has been disconnected." At first, I assumed the phone bill hadn't been paid or that it would be just a matter of hours or days at the most to reach them because this had happened before. After a week had passed without communication, I phoned my lawyer, his lawyer, his family, his friends and anyone else I could think that might know of their whereabouts. I got nothing.

As the second week began to pass, there was still no communication. Depression began to swallow me whole. The will to get out of bed every morning and go about my day was near impossible. One evening, an opportunity for me to be alone presented itself. This "storm" of brokenness, hopelessness, and despair literally brought me to my knees and to the feet of Jesus for redemption, reconciliation and salvation.

Without hope, I was on a mission to relieve my pain and misery. I had retrieved a bottle of prescription pills, a bottle of wine, paper, and a pen. I sat down and wrote goodbye letters to each of my children and to my parents. As I started to write to my dad, the whole "fatherly" concept came into focus more than ever before. After contemplating God, I spoke to Him. My conversation with Him started off with self-pity; then, it quickly surged into a full-blown assault on His good character for permitting me so much pain. I did what a lot of people do, rather than take any responsibility for my own worldly and selfish thoughts, behaviors, and choices; I passed the buck and pointed the blame on Him.

I have no idea how long this episode lasted, but it felt like an hour. When done, I sat slumped on the floor in sniffles, exhaustion, and for the first time ever - accountability. There was no one to blame for my predicament but myself. After this epitome of truth sank in, I begged God for His forgiveness with sincere humility and remorse.

3rd Sign – No Denial: Warmth filled the room and an intense amount of love enfolded me. When I looked up, a being of light stood before me and in that moment, I knew it was God. Purity and reverence radiated the room. He said, "Sweet child, I am here. I have always been here. It has been you who has turned your back from me always looking to the world or within yourself for answers. You have been calling and I have listened, now, it's your turn. Do what I say and all will be well."

After He faded away, the peace of love and solidity remained. I stood up, placed the pills back in the cabinet, lay the wine back in its rack, and trashed the letters that I had written. Feeling as if I had just come in from out in the rain, I took a long hot shower. That night, I washed off more than just the evening's emotional and physical sweat, dirt, and tears. I washed the stains of sin in my life down that drain and for the first time in my life, I felt free and loved. All I wanted to do was make Him proud. God had gained my complete and entire attention. If it were not for Him, I would be dead.

Two days later, the Lord blessed me with a phone call from my oldest son, David. He called to inform me that they had moved. I thanked God that it wasn't to the moon!

A vision: The next morning at 6:00 a.m., the alarm clock sounded. I hit the 'snooze' and fell back asleep. Ten minutes later, the alarm clock sounded again. I hit 'snooze' again and rolled back over to sleep some more, but this time, I did not experience the luxury of actual sleep; instead, I lay there with my eyes closed listening to sounds of the outdoors: dogs barking, birds tweeting, and squirrels running across the rooftop. I thought to myself, "Darn it! That alarm is going to go off again any minute." Just then, it sounded.

Somewhere between the seconds it took to raise my head from the pillow and open my eyes, the image "Corinthians 2, 3, 4, & 7" flashed across my mind. I had no idea what this message meant nor had I ever seen or heard of the word "Corinthians" ever before. It was a big word, a clear vision, and I was captivated.

I was mesmerized by the last few encounters and completed captured by the morning's vision. Later in the day, a client stopped me from styling her hair and gingerly asked, "What is wrong with you?"

I replied, "It's that noticeable?"

She nodded yes. To that retort, I leaned in close to her and whispered what happened just hours earlier. When I stepped back from her, she was smiling from ear to ear and with excitement she said, "Girrrrl, Corinthians is in the Book!"

The look of ignorance must have been on my face because after a momentary pause she said, "The

Bible Sweetheart. Stay here. I have one in my car. I'll go get it."

When she returned, she handed me the Bible and said, "Here, take it. It's yours."

Blessed with the vision and God's Word were when my thirst, hunger, and personal transformation in salvation truly evolved and has never stopped. My insignificant life – the "Patti Who?" phase – had meaning and purpose. Why it took me so long, especially after the divine healing of my son, only God truly knows. Aware that ultimate decisions in the end are mine, I had people of worldly persuasion still had a strong foothold in my life. In order to be obedient, I have to change the people with whom I kept close company with.

Both belief and believing in God brought an immense sense of knowledge like never before, but in the early stages of my conversion, I still occasionally leaned on my own understanding a little too much. But, as my faith grew, I learned to let go of worries and let God work His wonders.

My new state of enlightenment also brought forth a large spectrum of other enlightened people into my life. Not all of them were Christians. These various beliefs and theologies were very appealing because they made sense. Always curious, eager and desirous to confirm that the truth was in fact the truth, I dove into several metaphysical considerations from Buddhism to Humanism.

I practiced dousing, tarot, meditation and prayer. Bits and pieces of everything I was introduced to and practiced periodically attained me some incredible results; however, no matter what I did, I always found myself running back to the Bible and my relationship with Jesus Christ for answers and the wholeness, peace and unconditional love that no one and nothing else has given me.

Faith has taught me a lot about myself, life, and this world. To mention a few worldly facts, I have learned that when the ego gestures acts of kindness, it is only because it looks for acceptance, adoration, or control. I have learned that a person's affection, friendship, and loyalty usually come with a price. And, I have learned that the conscience is more comfortable to live life without a relationship with God because that is when our actions, thoughts, and choices are never accounted for.

Faith has taught me lessons about God, Jesus, His Spirit, and His heavenly ways. To mention a few, I have learned that God does not desire us to live in unrelenting pain. He does not want us morbidly fixated on what's wrong or missing. He does not want our hearts or minds closed-off to Him; and He does not wants us fixated on the dark and evilness of this world.

The Bible requests that we turn our other cheek when someone offends us, but this can be a terribly difficult reaction depending on the offense. The phrase, "An eye for an eye and a tooth for a tooth" not only carries retribution, it packs a powerful punch of insurmountable destruction that destroys lives, both theirs and yours. So, do not seek revenge. Take comfort in a thing called karma. Whether it is good or bad, a person's actions will come back on them tenfold and they will have to stand before God in judgment just as you and I will.

Through Christ, a Godly person disagrees with you and holds you accountable while unconditionally loving you at the same time. A Godly person is gentle and has good morals. A Godly person sees an issue from all perspectives and makes a proper choice without judging or condemning you or anyone else for that matter. They do all these things with unconditional love no matter how you respond.

As for relationship advice, contemplate on what the men and women within the previous pages of this book have had to say about their spouse and marriages because it is those who remove their eyes away from God and to the world that end in divorce. The successful marriages have God in their equation, they have a greater appreciation for life, they respect and honor each other, they protect one another, and they protect their relationship from outside influences, such as people as well as circumstances. They take each other's needs, feelings, and desires into themselves by silently doing ordinary things with an immense burning love that make their every gesture, step, word, and action redemptive.

For those who are married, be thankful for the days when you wake up pleased with one another, be thankful for your family and yourself, be thankful for communication and the times you can talk to and understand each other without saying a word, be thankful for companionship and the times when you can work together on projects that you both enjoy, be thankful for solitude, and be thankful for your times of relaxed freedom, personal trust, loyalty, and each other's individuality.

Who or what inspired me to write this book? *God.*

Out for dinner one night, I heard a man's voice from behind say, "You are going to write me a book." Slightly startled, I turned around to see who was behind me, but found no one. I shrugged that moment off because I thought that maybe I overheard a conversation from another table. So, I continued eating.

A few seconds later, I heard the voice again. As He spoke, I gained an immediate awareness of God's Presence. His message emanated immense love and warmth just like that life changing night at my apartment many years before. He said, "You are going to write a book sharing with the world the lives of My children. You are going to tell their stories of how they came into faith with Me, why they believe what they do, and what they know that so many others do not. Talk to the men because out of all My children, they have it the hardest."

Immediately, my mind went into prayer. I asked God for a sign to prove that who I heard was in fact Him and not my imagination. He gave me that sign just as I was leaving the restaurant parking lot.

As I was making my out of the lot and to the traffic light, a pick-up truck pulled just in front of me. It was a manly man's truck. Decked out with a lift kit, stack exhaust pipes, a gun rack along the back window, and stickers representing hunting, fishing, and diving, one sticker in particular stood out amongst the rest. A sticker in the center of the truck's back bumper read, "Real Men Love Christ!"

From that moment on, I began this journey on which the Lord has placed me and I haven't looked back. As for my faith, it deepens every day.

Many religions and practices claim Jesus as nothing more than a prophet. The Bible, The Word of God, claims Him to be God in flesh purposely sent to be sacrificed for our sins. When you take the time to read and truly reflect, all religion and practice do acknowledge Jesus as the only human being in the world who loved selflessly, performed miracles, and stood firm in faith even when he endured the torment of his pending death. He willingly chose to take on our sins, punishments, and deserving deaths. No one else in history or in any other religion is recorded to have ever made such a selfless act of love – ever! He is who the Bible claims Him to be.

To encounter God, talk to Him through prayer. Prayer is where your connection and communion with

Him tie together. Prayer is where your heart speaks to His heart in the privacy and reality of your current circumstance and, it is where your asking and His giving go hand in hand. When you come to Him in the name of Jesus, you come on the basis of who He is, not who you are and this is when your mountains of adversity move!

Allow God and His will to have free access into your life. He loves you more than you could ever love yourself; He understands you better than you could ever understand yourself and, He knows and wants what is best for you.

Faith pleases God. God keeps us from sin. God protects us from the enemy. God helps us find peace. God helps us find healing. God helps us live successfully and, God breaks down protective walls in our lives that actually lead to destruction. These are facts that I have learned first-hand when I have had moments of not remaining focused on Him. When I'm centered on Him, good choices are made and life is good.

Our actions must reflect our words which must reflect God's greatest attribute: love. Love one another no matter what because love is what softens a person's heart and hurt. This is the love that leads.

Words of Encouragement

"Although misconduct exists in this world, so does genuine love, respect, and appreciation. Do not allow your past predicaments, mistreatments, flawed choices, or other's condemning remarks keep you from becoming the best person you can be because no one is perfect.

"Look at the experienced conversions of men and women both past and present. Most of these people were fishermen, shepherds, and slaves, not politicians, millionaires, or dignitaries. Some of these people had a checkered past of murder, robbery, adultery, and prostitution. When they went to God and sought His forgiveness, God accepted them just as they were. He saw their worth just as He sees yours, He knew their heart just as He knows yours, and He knew their capability just as He knows yours. So, open your mind, open your heart, and invite Him to take up vacancy. Only He can clean up the debris and emotional scars of your past and present.

"I pray that this literature is a great experience for you – a gift – that makes you reflect on what's important and encourages both your growth and change. I pray that as you make your way through the minefields of this life, you remember to focus on your most important future of all - where you are going once you leave here.

"God bless you, and may His grace, mercy, love, and wisdom flow over you as you move into the Truth."

– Patricia Edwards

ENDORSEMENTS

"With insight and compassion Patricia Edwards tells of individuals whose lives got changed and empowered as a result of their encounter with the grace of Christ who reveals the love of God and results in the fellowship of the Holy Spirit. Drawing on many walks of life, Edwards provides a rich tapestry of what it means to live the life which is life, indeed!"
- **Hal Horan, retired pastor, having served churches in Michigan, Florida, Louisiana and Virginia**

"This collection of personal testimonies as told by Patricia Edwards is a good reminder to all of God's faithfulness and the power of salvation through Christ Jesus. Those searching for answers, as well as the new believer, will be especially inspired as Patricia leaves enough real life expressions (as told by those she interviewed) in her manuscript to speak to the human soul of those who will quickly identify with the fleshly struggles of living in today's world. Inspiring!"
- **Deborah Ross, President & Executive Director of Operations, Deborah Ross Ministries, Inc., Author, & Christian Speaker**

"In a world prevalent with struggles, this book gives people a chance to step away and remember that life can be good."
- **Elise Larsen, account specialist, Citgo Petroleum**

"The stories within this book will resonate with many readers in this day and age. Many will find the testimonies inspirational and possibly helpful with something they may be going through."
- **Chastity Bush, Romance Author**

"The testimonies are joyfully moving as they exhibit the realities of faith, the significance of Christ, the conversion of souls, and the detriment of those who keep their eyes and heart on the world."
- **Mitchell Estep, project director and retired Special Forces**

"The heart of this writer is to be rewarded. The stories shared are soul warming as they reveal God's marvelous grace and abounding love for us. This is a guide book that will lead to buried treasure. When you find the treasure you will smile, cry, shout and rejoice."
- **Dr. Ron Elville, Pastor/counselor**